The Christmas Story:
What Really Happened
By Dr. Chuck Missler

Koinonia House

The Christmas Story: What Really Happened
© Copyright 2015 Koinonia House Inc.
Published by Koinonia House
P.O. Box D
Coeur d'Alene, ID 83816-0347
www.khouse.org

ISBN: 978-1-57821-638-3

All Rights Reserved.
No portion of this book may be reproduced in any form whatsoever without the written permission of the Publisher.

All Scripture quotations are from the King James Version of the Holy Bible.

PRINTED IN THE UNITED STATES OF AMERICA

Table of Contents

Introduction *1*

When Was Jesus Born? 3
4 B.C.? *3*
2 B.C.? *4*
John the Baptist to the Rescue *5*
Why December 25th as the Birth Date of Jesus? .. *8*

Babylonian Traditions 9
The Tammuz Legend *11*
The Messianic Promise *13*

The Genealogy of Christ 17
Sevens in the Bible *17*
The Two Genealogies *21*
The Book of Ruth *24*

An Integrated Design 41
The Authentication of Christ *41*

History of the Magi 43
Alexander the Great *46*
The Roman Empire and the Parthians *49*
The Visit of the Magi *51*
Traditions and the Magi *55*

To Egypt and Nazareth 61
Rabbi Yitzhak Kaduri *63*
Herod and the Babies of Bethlehem *67*
The Branch *69*

The Mazzaroth and the Zodiac 71

Egypt and Ethiopia 75
The Scepter has Departed from Judah *79*
Review of Major Lessons *80*
Psalm 69: The Silent Years in the Life of Christ .. *81*
Our Coming King *87*

Endnotes 93

Introduction

Almost everyone throughout the world celebrates Christmas. Christians celebrate Christmas as the birth of Jesus Christ, and we celebrate it on December 25. But is that really the birth date of Christ? Or was it on September 29, 2 B.C.? We are going on a genealogical treasure hunt and we will also explore a number of topics relevant to Christ's birth. The first element we must consider is a genealogy—the genealogy of Christ. Genealogies are lists in the Bible that many of us skip over, and yet it is astonishing what they will reveal to the diligent student.

There are important questions that need to be answered. When was Jesus born? Why a virgin birth? Why was He born in Bethlehem? What makes Bethlehem so special? These are all topics we will explore. There is also a great amount of tradition attached to the birth of Christ. It is so entrenched that even textbooks are full of traditions rather than data.

Chapter 1
When Was Jesus Born?

Most serious Bible students realize that Jesus was probably *not* born on December 25. Since the Bible doesn't explicitly identify the birthday of our Lord, many scholars have developed diverse opinions as to the likely birthday of Jesus. Just what do we know about the time when Jesus was born? We know that the flocks were in an open field (Luke 2:8). That means it was not after October, because it would have been too cold. We also know that no competent Roman administrator would require registration involving travel during a season when Judea is hard to travel through and generally impassable (Matthew 24:20). Therefore, we know the time of year was not in the winter.

4 B.C.?

It is commonly presumed that Jesus was born in 4 B.C. But, this date is primarily from erroneous conclusions made by Josephus. He recorded an eclipse that was assumed to be on March 13, 4 B.C., just before Herod died. Other scholars believe that the eclipse occurred on December 29, 1 B.C.

Irenaeus, a noted apologist, was born about a century after Jesus, and he also notes that the Lord was born in the 41st year of the reign of Augustus.

We also know that considerable time elapsed between Jesus' birth and Herod's death since the family fled to Egypt to escape Herod's edict to slaughter the babes in Bethlehem. They did not return until after Herod's death (Matthew 2:15; 19-22).

According to the *Magillath Ta'anith*, an ancient Jewish scroll contemporary with Jesus, Herod died on January 14, 1 B.C. (there is no "0" year Between B.C. and A.D.).

2 B.C.?

Tertullian (born about 160 A.D.) stated that Augustus began to rule forty-one years before the birth of Jesus and died fifteen years after that event, on August 19, 14 A.D.[1] Since Augustus began his reign in the autumn of 43 B.C., this also appears to substantiate the birthdate of 2 B.C. for Christ.

Tertullian also notes that Jesus was born twenty-eight years after the death of Cleopatra (30 B.C.), which is also consistent with a date of 2 B.C.

Eusebius (264 A.D.-340 A.D.), the Father of Church History, ascribes the birth to the 42nd year of the reign of Augustus and the 28th year from the subjection of Egypt upon the death of Anthony and Cleopatra.[2] The 42nd year of Augustus began in the autumn of 1 B.C. The subjugation of Egypt by the Roman Empire occurred in the autumn of 30 B.C., sometime after the Battle of Actium. The 28th year extended from the autumn of 3 B.C. to the autumn of 2 B.C. Therefore, the only date that would meet both of these constraints would be the autumn of 2 B.C.

John the Baptist to the Rescue

At this point, the circumstances surrounding the birth of John the Baptist provide some help. Elisabeth, John's mother, was a cousin of Mary and the wife of a priest named Zacharias who was of the *course,* or priestly order, of Abijah (Luke 1:5; 8-13; 23, 24). During the reign of King David, the priests were divided into twenty-four courses and each course officiated in the Temple for one week, from Sabbath to Sabbath. The course of Abijah was the eighth course, according to 1 Chronicles 24:10.

(7) Now the first lot came forth to Jehoiarib, the second to Jedaiah,
(8) The third to Harim, the fourth to Seorim,
(9) The fifth to Malchijah, the sixth to Mijamin,
(10) The seventh to Hakkoz, the eighth to Abijah,
(11) The ninth to Jeshua, the tenth to Shecaniah,
(12) The eleventh to Eliashib, the twelfth to Jakim,
(13) The thirteenth to Huppah, the fourteenth to Jeshebeab,
(14) The fifteenth to Bilgah, the sixteenth to Immer,

(15) The seventeenth to Hezir, the eighteenth to Aphses,
(16) The nineteenth to Pethahiah, the twentieth to Jehezekel,
(17) The one and twentieth to Jachin, the two and twentieth to Gamul,
(18) The three and twentieth to Delaiah, the four and twentieth to Maaziah.
(19) These were the orderings of them in their service to come into the house of the LORD, according to their manner, under Aaron their father, as the LORD God of Israel had commanded him.

1 Chronicles 24:7-19

The Talmud and Josephus both record that the Temple was destroyed by Titus on August 5, 70 A.D., and the first course of priests had just taken office. Tracking backwards, Zacharias would have ended his duties on July 13, 3 B.C. If the birth of John the Baptist took place 280 days later (normal gestation time for a child), he would have been born on April 19-20, 2 B.C. (which was Passover of that year). Assuming John was born on April 19-20, 2 B.C., his 30th birthday would have been April 19-20, 29 A.D., in the 15th year of Tiberius. Numbers 4:3 tells us that the minimum age for the ministry was thirty. So John began his ministry in the 15th year of Tiberius Caesar, 28 A.D.

> *Now in the fifteenth year of the reign of Tiberius Caesar, Pontius Pilate being governor of Judaea, and Herod being tetrarch of Galilee, and his*

brother Philip tetrarch of Ituraea and of the region of Trachonitis, and Lysanias the tetrarch of Abilene,
Luke 3:1

As Augustus died on August 19, 14 A.D., that was the accession year for Tiberius. All of this seems to confirm the 2 B.C. date for the birth of Jesus and, since John the Baptist was six months older than Jesus, this also confirms an autumn birth date for Jesus. John the Baptist's repeated introduction of Jesus as the Lamb of God (John 1:29-30) is particularly interesting if John was indeed born on Passover.

Scripture states that Elisabeth hid herself for five months (Luke 1:25) and then the Archangel Gabriel announced to Mary both Elisabeth's condition and that Mary also would bear a son who would be called Jesus. The Apostle Luke records that Mary went "with haste" to visit Elisabeth—who was then in the first week of her sixth month, which was the fourth week of December in 3 B.C.

And, behold, thy cousin Elisabeth, she hath also conceived a son in her old age: and this is the sixth month with her, who was called barren.
Luke 1:36

If Jesus was born 280 days later, it would place the date of his birth on September 29, 2 B.C. That would have been on the day of the Feast of Trumpets in that year.[3] We realize all these things are speculative but they are intended to stretch the imagination away from the traditions. What's the correct date? No one knows for sure.

Why December 25th as the Birth Date of Jesus?

The early church did not celebrate Christ's birth. In fact, the Jewish tradition was to celebrate the death of a person, not the birth. The first recorded mention of December 25 is in the Calendar of Philocalus (354 A.D.), which assumed Jesus' birth to be a Friday, December 25, 1 A.D. Incidentally, December 25, 1 A.D. was not on a Friday. With the Edict of Toleration (312 A.D.), the Emperor Constantine legalized Christianity; the persecuted Christians exchanged the rags of hiding in the caves for the silks of the court. Christianity became official, therefore, in 312 A.D.

Constantine recognized there was a huge population of slaves in the Roman Empire, and over half of them were Christians. Making Christianity legal was a very shrewd political move. Of course, as time went on, many of the previous pagan rituals were adapted to fit the new "Christian" trappings.

The date of December 25th was officially proclaimed by the church fathers in 440 A.D. This date was actually a vestige of the Roman holiday of Saturnalia, observed near the winter solstice[4] (shortest day and longest night of the year), which itself was among the many pagan traditions inherited from the earlier Babylonian priesthood. The sun god was thought to have died on the winter solstice.

Chapter 2
Babylonian Traditions

Virtually all occultic traditions have had their origins in the original city of Babylon (Isaiah 47). That priestly system from Babylon then moved to Persepolis during the era of the Persians and ultimately found itself in Rome. Virtually everything in pagan Rome consisted of Babylonian practices with a Latin name. It has been the continued adherence to these idolatrous influences that has evoked the intense criticism of Roman Catholicism by Protestants over many centuries.

All of this began with Bab-El, or Babylon, which has over 300 references to it in the Bible, and it is mentioned four times in Christ's genealogy (Matthew 1:1-17). The tower of Bab-El was Nimrod's (a descendant of Ham) centerpiece of his rebellion against God (Genesis 10). In a sense, the whole Bible is a saga between two cities: the City of God, called Jerusalem, and the city of man, or Satan, called Babylon. They both start in Genesis and they both climax in the Book of Revelation.

Bab-El has great meaning. *Bab* is the term for "gate or tower" and *El* is the term for God. Bab-El is the "tower to God" or the "gateway to the gods."

This is where we have God Himself intervening, causing the confusion of the tongues which occurs in Genesis 11. Not only was there a confusion of tongues, but the Mazzaroth (what we know as the "Zodiac") was corrupted. It was in Babylon that the original concepts became distorted.

Babylon figures prominently in history and in prophecy. From the perspective of prophecy, Babylon is presently being rebuilt 100 kilometers (62 miles) south of Baghdad. Babylon is destined for a rebirth, and she will eventually receive the judgment that is explicitly described in Isaiah and Jeremiah.

> *And Babylon, the glory of kingdoms, the beauty of the Chaldees' excellency, shall be as when God overthrew Sodom and Gomorrah.*
>
> Isaiah 13:19

> *And saying, Alas, alas, that great city, that was clothed in fine linen, and purple, and scarlet, and decked with gold, and precious stones, and pearls!*
>
> Revelation 18:16

> *And they cast dust on their heads, and cried, weeping and wailing, saying, Alas, alas, that great city, wherein were made rich all that had ships in the sea by reason of her costliness! for in one hour is she made desolate.*
>
> Revelation 18:19

This may be a contemporary "litmus test" for taking prophecies literally, but as yet there is no evidence of this occurring. However, if we understand the Bible correctly, it would seem that there is a huge destiny yet ahead for this fabled city.[5]

The Tammuz Legend

In order to understand the origin of the various occultic practices of Babylon, we need to look at the original city and the story of Tammuz, the son of Nimrod (the founder of Babylon) and his queen, Semiramis. Tammuz was identified with the Babylonian sun god and was worshipped following the winter solstice, which is around December 22-23. Tammuz was thought to have died during this time, and this was memorialized by burning a log in the fireplace. The Chaldean word for "infant" is "yule."[6] His "rebirth" was celebrated by replacing the log with a trimmed tree the following morning. So what we think of today as a Christmas tree actually had its roots in Babylon. Jeremiah 10 states the following:

Thus saith the Lord, Learn not the way of the heathen, and be not dismayed at the signs of heaven; for the heathen are dismayed at them. For the customs of the people are vain: for one cutteth a tree out of the forest, the work of the hands of the workmen with the ax. They deck it with silver and with gold; they fasten it with nails and with hammers that it move not. They are upright as the palm tree, but speak not: they must needs be borne, because they cannot go. Be not afraid of them; for they cannot do evil, neither also is it in them to do good.

Jeremiah 10: 2-5

In all candor, Jeremiah is talking about idol worship, a different thing altogether. Actually, the intent here is not to disdain the use of a Christmas tree, but rather to really understand the origins of some of our western traditions, including the Christmas tree.

When Christianity was established as the state religion of Rome, many of the previous religious traditions and practices of the earlier pagan worship were adapted and incorporated, including the Christmas tree, the mistletoe (a fertility symbol), the wassail bowl, and others. Again, all these things have their roots, strangely enough, in Babylon.

Many of our other holidays have their origins in ancient cultures. Perhaps one of the biggest of these is Halloween, which is clearly occultic. The Celts, the Druids, and many others observed October 31st [the Eve of Sahmain (Summer's End)—pronounced "sow-ween"] as the end of the year. All of this is related to the planet Mars, called Baal, which may very likely have been interfering with the orbit of the earth on some previous occasions.[7]

Easter is a holiday that retains its original pagan name. This celebration originally involved the worship of Ishtar, the Golden Egg of Astarte, and was held with all kinds of fertility rites in the spring. Prolific rabbits are a major symbol of fertility and that is how the rabbits got commingled with the eggs.

It is an interesting fact that the early Christians who attempted to worship Passover in accordance with the instructions in the Bible were excommunicated from the church and called the *quartodecimens*.[8]

The Messianic Promise

In Genesis 3:15, God declares war on the *Nahash*, Satan, the Shining One, and there He announces for the first time in the written Scriptures the promise of the kinsman-redeemer (Jesus Christ), who will come from the line of Adam.

Satan understands that there is a war going on. He has continually attempted to eradicate the Messianic line from Eve onwards throughout history, even to today. Satan has attempted to interrupt the royal line from Cain and Abel to the Flood of Noah; from the slaughter of the infants in Egypt in the Book of Exodus, all the way to the slaughter of the babes in Bethlehem.

After the death of Abel, Satan tried to corrupt the human line with the shenanigans of the fallen angels in Genesis 6, attacking Abraham's seed in Genesis 12 and Genesis 20, the famine in Genesis 50, the destruction of the male line in Exodus 1, and Pharaoh's pursuit of the Hebrew nation (Exodus 14), which culminated with the destruction of Pharaoh's army, and the populating of Canaan.

Before Abraham's people returned from Egypt, Satan had four centuries to lay down a minefield, and that is why Joshua is instructed to wipe out every man, woman and child of certain tribes. As God revealed

His plan more clearly, Satan focused his attack more tightly. God revealed that the Messiah would not only come from the line of Abraham, He would also come from the line of David. So, the family of David was singled out by Satan from 2 Samuel onwards. And all through here, we find him trying to kill all the heirs to the throne. But there was always one; one hidden by a servant or saved in some other way—and that kept the line going. The attacks on David's line included:

Jehoram killed his brothers in 2 Chronicles 21
Arabians slew all but Ahazariah
    in 2 Chronicles 21
Athaliah killed all but Joash in 2 Chronicles 22
Hezekiah assaulted, etc. in Isaiah 36, 38
Haman's attempt to kill all Jews in Esther 3

We notice this attempt to wipe out the Jews in the Book of Esther, when Haman, emboldened by Satan, devised a plan for their extinction. Satan's other attacks were focused on key families; this attack was to be a wholesale massacre.

When we move into the New Testament, the stratagems of Satan continue:

Joseph's fear for Mary in Matthew 1
Herod's murder attempts in Matthew 2
Men at the synagogue in Nazareth in Luke 4
Two storms on the Sea in Mark 4; Luke 8
The Cross in Matthew 27; Mark 15; Luke 23; John 19
The Dragon in Revelation 12

In fact, Revelation 12 is a summary of Satan's stratagems, and yet he is not through. Throughout history there has been extreme prejudice against the Jews, and we are seeing it even in our time.

Chapter 3
The Genealogy of Christ

When we go back to the birth of Christ and His genealogy, it is full of surprises. It is protected with a security system written into the text. There is an authentication code which acts like an automatic security monitor, and it watches every little letter of the text. The system never wears out, and it has been running continually for several thousand years. This is the fingerprint signature of the Author and it is designed to avoid compromise.

Sevens in the Bible

Sevens occur in over 600 passages in the Bible. Many of them are implicit, some are very overt, and some are very structural, hidden under the text. That underlying heptadic (sevenfold) structure of the text can serve as a fingerprint of the Author.

To illustrate this, try to create a fictitious genealogy. This can be the genealogy of anyone, but there are a few rules:

— The number of **words** you use must be divisible by 7 exactly
— The number of **letters** you use must be divisible by 7 exactly

— The number of **vowels** must be divisible by 7 exactly
— The number of **consonants** must be divisible by 7 exactly
— The number of words that **begin with a vowel** must be divisible by 7 exactly
— The number of words that **begin with a consonant** must be divisible by 7 exactly

Now, if you have only one rule, you have one chance in seven of getting it right. If you have two rules, and you just do it by random chance, you will have one chance in 49 of getting it right. But now we have more rules.

The number of words that:

— **occur more than once** must be divisible by 7
— **occur in more than one form** must be divisible by 7
— **occur in only one form** must be divisible by 7

And just a few more rules for your genealogy:
— **The number of nouns** shall be divisible by 7
— **Only 7 words shall not be nouns**
— The **number of names** shall be divisible by 7
— Only **7 other kinds of nouns are permitted**
— The **number of male names** shall be divisible by 7
— The **number of generations** shall be divisible by 7

Okay, that's probably enough rules. This is a description of the genealogy of Jesus Christ as found in the first eleven verses of Matthew. And all of this has to be in the Greek language which is probably the most precise, rigid language ever written, and each letter has its own Greek alphanumeric number.[9]

Greek Alphanumerics

α	1	κ	10	ρ	100
β	2	κ	20	σ ς	200
γ	3	λ	30	τ	300
δ	4	μ	40	υ	400
ε	5	ν	50	φ	500
ς*	6	ξ	60	χ	600
ζ	7	ο	70	ψ	700
η	8	π	80	ω	800
θ	9	ϙ*	90	§*	900

*Vau(6), Koppa(90), and samsi(900), later became extinct.

The chart below shows that with just nine rules for this genealogy, there is only one chance in over 40 million of creating this genealogy by random chance.

Chances of Multiples of 7	
For 2 7^2=7x7	49
For 3 7^3=7x7x7	343
For 4 7^4=7x7x7x7	2,401
For 5 7^5	16,807
For 6 7^6	117,649
For 7 7^7	823,543
For 8 7^8	5,794,801
For 9 7^9	40,353,607

Now, as amazing as that is, there is even more. In the rest of Matthew 1 there are 161 words, and they also maintain a very elaborate heptadic structure underneath the text.

So how long would it take for someone to construct such a genealogy? Assume they will work eight hours a day, 40 hours a week, 50 weeks a year, and have two weeks off for Christmas. That will be 2,000 hours, man-hours, per week, or 120,000 minutes per year.

The number of attempts needed, if this is randomized, would be 7 to the 9th power, or 7^9. That would be over 40 million attempts.

Say it would take an average of ten minutes to try one draft; that would be 403 million minutes. This little project will take about 3,000 years of work.

This is laid out just to demonstrate that anyone who would say the probability of this happening by a statistical randomness is incredibly naïve. Some scribe didn't sit down and go through these calculations to make it come out that way.

These discoveries were actually made by Dr. Ivan Panin, and he is famous for this very thing—the hepatic structures underlying the Biblical text. Dr. Panin was born in Russia in 1855, immigrated to the United States at an early age, and graduated from Harvard with a PhD in mathematics. In 1882, he became a Christian. When he discovered the heptadic structures of the text, he spent the remainder of his life (fifty years) generating 43,000 pages of discoveries. He went to be with the Lord in 1943.

The Two Genealogies

The Bible provides us with two lengthy genealogies of Christ. Matthew, as a Levite, focuses on the Messiahship of Jesus in that he traces the legal line from Abraham (thought to be the first Jew) through David, then Solomon and the royal line, to Joseph, the legal father of Jesus (Matthew 1:1-17) and the husband of Mary. Luke, as a physician, focuses on the humanity of Jesus. He traces the blood line from Adam (the Son of God versus us, the sons of Adam) and once Luke gets to Abraham, the genealogy is identical to Matthew's up to the House of David. Then Luke goes from David, through Nathan (a different son of David) to Mary, the mother of Jesus (Luke 3:23-38).

Let's take a look at the last ten people mentioned at the end of Luke 3:

which was the son of Noe, which was the son of Lamech, Which was the son of Mathusala, which was the son of Enoch, which was the son of Jared, which was the son of Maleleel, which was the son of Cainan, Which was the son of Enos, which was the son of Seth, which was the son of Adam, which was the son of God.

Luke 3:36d-38

If we translate those names from their Hebrew roots they will spell out a sentence. In other words, there is a hidden message in this genealogy.

A Hidden Message

Adam	Man (is)
Seth	Appointed
Enosh	Mortal
Kenan	Sorrow, (but)
Mahalalel	The Blessed God
Jared	Shall come down
Enoch	Teaching
Methuselah	His death shall bring
Lamech	The despairing
Noah	Comfort, Rest

When all of that is put together, we have a summary of the Christian Gospel hidden away in the genealogy of the Torah: **Man is appointed mortal sorrow** but **the blessed God shall come down teaching** that **His death shall bring** the **despairing comfort or rest.**

Look more closely and see Who's death is being predicted. It is God's death.

All of this tells us that there is more going on here than just a simple list of family names. The entire thing is being designed with a profound end in view.

After Luke, we switch to Matthew.

The Birth of Jesus fulfilled the following Specifications:

Specifications Fulfilled

He would be born of a virgin	*Isaiah 7:14*
And He was!	*-Matt. 1:18-25*
He would be born in Bethlehem	*Micah 5:2*
And He was!	*-Matt. 2:1-6*
He would be taken into Egypt	*Hosea 11:1*
And He was!	*-Matt. 2:15*
He would heal and make people whole	*Isaiah 53*
And He did!	*-Matt. 8*
He would be crucified	*Psalm 22:14-17*
And He was!	*-Matt. 27:31*
He would die for our sins	*Isaiah 53*
And He did!	*-John 11:49-52*
He would rise from the dead	*Psalm 16:10*
And He did!	*-Matt. 28:1-10*

He had the most distinguished Family Tree in history:

— Encrypted in the Torah in Genesis 38
— Prophesied in Judges and Ruth 4
— Evades the blood curse on Jeconiah in Jeremiah 22:20
— Virgin Birth in Genesis 3:15; Isaiah 7:14 Psalm 69; Psalm 110

The Book of Ruth

Another amazing story about the genealogy of Jesus is in the Book of Ruth. When we carefully study Ruth and Genesis we discover that Boaz, Obed, Jesse, and David have all been prophesied in both books.

Why was Jesus born in Bethlehem? The Book of Ruth is especially important to us at Christmas because it answers that question. Bethlehem was established as the "House of David" because of the events in the Book of Ruth. That designation had implications for Joseph and Mary when Caesar Augustus ordered a special tax to be levied.

And all went to be taxed, every one into his own city. And Joseph also went up from Galilee, out of the city of Nazareth, into Judaea, unto the city of David, which is called Bethlehem; (because he was of the house and lineage of David:) To be taxed with Mary his espoused wife, being great with child.

Luke 2:3-5

Bethlehem is where the shepherds were in their fields on that momentous night:

And there were in the same country shepherds abiding in the field, keeping watch over their flock by night. And, lo, the angel of the Lord came upon them, and the glory of the Lord shone round about them: and they were sore afraid.

Luke 2:8-9

Many believe (including the author) that those fields were the fields of Boaz and Ruth, so even their fields played a part in the birth of Christ.

Ruth is the ultimate love story in many ways. It is studied in some college classes just as an elegant piece of literature quite apart from its supernatural origin. At the literary level it is much respected. But at the prophetic and personal levels it can have a profound impact on every one of us. It is one of the most significant books of the Old Testament for the church.

The Book of Ruth profiles the role of the *kinsman-redeemer* and is often regarded as an essential prerequisite to understanding Revelation 5. It can often be difficult to comprehend that you and I are the beneficiaries of a love story that was written in blood on a wooden cross erected in Judea some 2,000 years ago. However, knowing the story of Ruth and the ramifications of that book, brings the sacrifice of Jesus, our Kinsman-Redeemer, into sharper focus.

In Ruth, we have this interesting case where a Gentile daughter-in-law, after the death of her husband, insists upon clinging to her Jewish mother-in-law. Numerous events occur prior to a famous scene on the threshing floor where Ruth makes the request of Boaz, a rich land owner, to take her as his bride.

The major scene occurs in chapter four when Boaz confronts the relative who's in the way of the marriage and the return of the land. This "nearer" kinsman was willing to redeem the property, but not willing to take Ruth as a bride. So he yields his shoe[10] to relinquish his right of redemption. Then Boaz steps up, purchases the land for Naomi, and purchases Ruth as a bride.

As they celebrate this romantic end of this love story, there is a comment made at the wedding, "May your house be like Pharez." At first glance, this sounds like a lovely toast at a wedding. However, the Bible has a difference perspective on it, which we will examine more closely later. The Book of Ruth provides us with a perfect outline, chapter by chapter:

The Kinsman-Redeemer

To the Greek (or Western) mind, prophecy is a prediction and a fulfillment. To the Jewish mind, prophecy is a pattern, or type. In the situation with Ruth, Boaz is acting as a kinsman-redeemer, and that role required that four conditions be met:

— He had to be a kinsman.
— He had to be able to perform the redemption.
— He had to be willing to do it.
— He had to assume all the obligations.

That is exactly what Boaz ends up doing for Ruth and Naomi, and that is exactly what Christ does for us.

— He had to be a kinsman of Adam, a human being.
— He had to be sinless in order to be able to perform the redemption.
— He had to be willing to do it. Gethsemane shows this was true.
— He also had to assume all the obligations. He has made us the people of God.

So, Boaz is the lord of the harvest and the kinsman-redeemer in the story, and he also typologically represents our Kinsman-Redeemer, Jesus Christ. Naomi is the symbol of Israel who has lost her land, but through Boaz's act of redemption she is returned to her land. And Ruth is his Gentile bride. All of this makes the parallelism very real.

Another interesting fact about this story is that the reading of the Book of Ruth is always associated with the Feast of Shavuot, the Feast of Weeks or the Feast of Pentecost, the very feast that celebrates the birth of the church.

As we continue to examine the Book of Ruth, we notice several instructive points:

— Ruth, a Gentile, does not replace Naomi, an Israelite.
— Ruth learns of Boaz's ways through Naomi.
— Naomi meets Boaz through Ruth.

— Boaz loved Ruth, but he had to await her move
— Boaz, not Ruth, confronts the nearer kinsman (Deuteronomy 25:5-10)[11]
— The Book of Ruth is always read at the Feast of Shavuot

The Strange Prophecy

There is also a very strange prophecy in the Book of Ruth:

And let thy house be like the house of Pharez, whom Tamar bare unto Judah, of the seed which the LORD shall give thee of this young woman.

Ruth 4:12

This sordid tale goes back to Genesis 38, where Tamar is forced to contrive an illegitimate son from Judah, her father-in-law, in order to continue the messianic line. She gave birth to twins, and the one connected to the Book of Ruth is Pharez (Perez), who was considered illegitimate. It would be a disdainful thing for someone at the wedding to say, "May your house be like Pharez" because most everyone there would know about Perez as well as the Law:

A bastard shall not enter into the congregation of the LORD; even to his tenth generation shall he not enter into the congregation of the LORD.

Deuteronomy 23:2

Boaz was in the seventh generation after Perez. Ruth 4:18 has the genealogy after Perez—Hezron,

Ram, Amninadab, Nashon, Salmon, Boaz, Obed, Jesse, and David. David is the tenth generation. God had planned for David to be king from the beginning. But the line had to be cleared for ten generations before David could come forth. In fact, the "tenth man" in the Old Testament is always very relevant.

The Tenth Man

Adam	Shem	Isaac	Perez
Seth	Arphaxad	Jacob	Hezron
Enosh	Salah	Judah	Ram
Kenan	Eber	Perez	Amminadab
Mahalalel	Peleg	Hezron	Nahson
Jared	Rue	Ram	Salmon
Enoch	Serug	Amminadab	Boaz
Methuselah	Nahor	Nashon	Obed
Lamech	Terah	Salmon	Jesse
Noah	**Abraham**	**Boaz**	**David**

This was prophesied long, long before even the days of Boaz and Ruth. In fact, look at another section of Genesis 38, the very heart of the Torah. In the Hebrew text, at 49-letter intervals, the name "Boaz" appears.

Using this pattern of a 49-letter interval for each letter, we also find the name "Ruth."

Following her name, at a 49-letter interval, is the name "Obed," and then "Yishay" (Jesse), and then again, continuing, there is the name of "David."

So here we have Boaz, Ruth, Obed, Jesse, and David in 49-letter intervals, all in chronological order, hidden in the text. Statistically, the likelihood of this happening by accident or chance is absurd. This is by design.

What is even more bizarre about this design is that it is in the Book, it's in the Torah, the five books of Moses, long before Joshua, before Judges, even before Samuel the prophet, who anointed David (1 Samuel 16:13). David is a very key figure in all of these things.

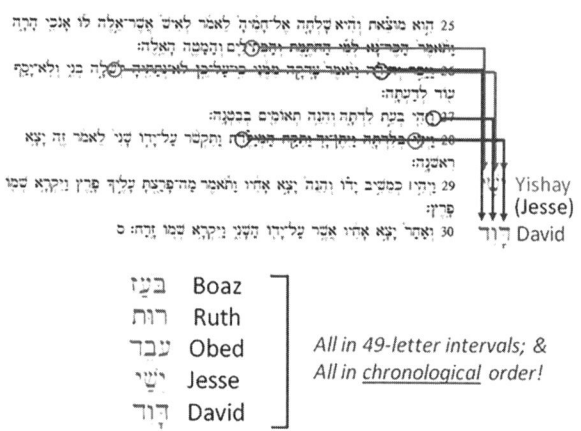

All in 49-letter intervals; & All in <u>chronological</u> order!

Let's take a more extensive look at the House of David. Matthew, being a Jew, began the genealogy of Jesus with Abraham. Then he goes through to David, Solomon, and on to Josiah and Jehoiakim. To really understand this, we need to back up and look at some history.

After Solomon died, the nation split into two houses: northern (Israel) and southern (Judea). The northern house went through nine different dynasties, each going from bad to worse and finally obliterated from history under the Assyrian invasion. The southern house had only one dynasty, the Davidic dynasty. Due to God's commitment and covenant to David, there is only the one dynasty for the Jews, and it is perpetual.

Of course, some of the specific kings in that dynasty were chastised when they did not perform well, such as Ahaziah, Joash, and Amaziah--who all died violent deaths. God was thus dealing with idolatry literally "to the third and fourth generations" (Exodus 20:4, 5). Their names therefore were "blotted out" according to the Law (Deuteronomy 29:20). However, the Davidic dynasty stayed intact. When the royal line got to Jehoiachin (also called Jeconiah or Coniah), things had gotten so bad that God pronounced a blood curse on him.

The Blood Curse

> *Thus saith the LORD, Write ye this man childless, a man that shall not prosper in his days: for no man of his seed shall prosper, sitting upon the throne of David, and ruling any more in Judah.*
>
> Jeremiah 22:30

This is just amazing! When God pronounced this blood curse, there must have been a celebration in the councils of Satan because, from Satan's point of view,

God has put himself in a contradiction. God indicated in Genesis 49 that the Messiah was going to come from the tribe of Judah and specifically from the line of David. Then God pronounced a blood curse on that royal line that "no man of his seed shall prosper sitting upon the throne of David and ruling any more in Judah." God's adversaries must have been overjoyed at this. Just imagine, at this point, God turning to the angels and saying, "Watch this one."

Pay close attention, now, because this can get complicated. The Matthew account goes down through Jehoiachin and finally gets to Joseph, who is the "legal" father of Jesus Christ. He is in the legal line of the house of David.

> *And Jacob begat Joseph the husband of Mary, of whom was born Jesus, who is called Christ.*
>
> Matthew 1:16

Joseph was "the husband of Mary," not the father of Jesus Christ, except in a legal sense.

To completely understand what is going to happen here, one needs to understand an exception in the Torah that was made for the daughters of Zelophehad.

How incredible that every detail—even in the regulations of the Torah—are there by deliberate design and always point to Christ. There is a peculiar exception recorded in the Torah, the result of a petition by the daughters of Zelophehad which provided for inheritance through the daughter, if no sons were available and she married within her tribe[12]. It became traditional, in such cases, that the father would legally adopt his son-in-law[13].

Just to be clear, this exception provided for the husband to become the "son" of the father–of–the–bride. And this exception anticipates the lineage of Jesus Christ. It also gives credence to the concept that every detail in the Bible is not only there by design, but also impacts directly the Messiah and the Messiahship. Joseph was the son-in-law of Heli, the father of Mary. In Luke 3:23, the word that is used in the Greek is the proper usage of the verb, *nomizo,* which means "reckoned as by law." The way *nomizo* should be translated is, "Joseph was the son-in-law of Heli" (by legal adoption).

The Virgin Birth

This miraculous event was hinted at in the Garden of Eden when God speaks of the Redeemer as "the seed of the woman…" (Genesis 3:15). That becomes a title of Jesus Christ. It was prophesied by Isaiah:

> *Therefore the Lord himself shall give you a sign; Behold, a virgin shall conceive, and bear a son, and shall call his name Immanuel.*
>
> Isaiah 7:14

Some skeptics quibble about the Hebrew word for "virgin" in verse 14. It is *ha alma* meaning "the virgin"; this is not just any virgin, but *the* virgin. Some say that it can mean just a young maid. If that were the case, how could that be "a sign"? Almost any young maid could conceive and bear a son. The context is clear that it means "a virgin." In fact, in the Septuagint, three centuries before Christ was born, the Jewish translators used the Greek term *parthenos*, which means clearly, specifically, and scientifically "a virgin." Those Hebrew experts, greater scholars than the modern skeptics, translated the Hebrew word *ha alma, virgin,* so that it is absolutely unambiguous.

The Isaiah prophecy is presented in Matthew as being fulfilled:

> *Now the birth of Jesus Christ was on this wise: When as his mother Mary was espoused to Joseph, before they came together, she was found with child of the Holy Ghost. Then Joseph her husband, being a just man, and not willing to make her a publick example, was minded to put her away privily.*
>
> Matthew 1:18-19

Joseph was concerned about Mary being stoned, as that was the punishment for adultery in those days.

> *But while he thought on these things, behold, the angel of the Lord appeared unto him in a dream, saying, Joseph, thou son of David, fear not to take unto thee Mary thy wife: for that which is conceived in her is of the Holy Ghost. And she shall bring forth a son, and thou shalt call his name JESUS: for he shall save his people from their sins. Now all this was done, that it might be fulfilled which was spoken of the Lord by the prophet,*

*saying, Behold, a virgin shall be with child,
and shall bring forth a son, and they shall call his
name Emmanuel, which being interpreted is,
God with us.*

Matthew 1:20-23

The blood curse from Jeremiah 22 is closely tied to this issue. In fact, when we examine closely the blood curse on the royal line, the virgin birth becomes a requirement. Notice that the genealogy given in Luke comes down through Heli, who is the father-in-law of Joseph. Jesus Christ, the Messiah, is of the House and lineage of David: of the House of David legally, and of the lineage by blood. That lineage is not the bloodline through Solomon, but through Nathan, the second surviving son of David and Bathsheba. In other words, Luke takes a left turn and goes to another son—not Solomon, but Nathan.[14]

In order to provide some additional background, look at Isaiah 7:10-13:

*Moreover the LORD spake again unto Ahaz,
saying, Ask thee a sign of the LORD thy God;
ask it either in the depth, or in the height above.
But Ahaz said, I will not ask, neither will I tempt
the LORD. And he said, Hear ye now, O house of
David; Is it a small thing for you to weary men,
but will ye weary my God also? Therefore the Lord
himself shall give you a sign; Behold, a virgin shall
conceive, and bear a son, and shall call his name
Immanuel.*[15]

Isaiah 7:10-14

This is a challenge, a dare that Ahaz decides to defer. God shifts and gives the sign, not to Ahaz, but to the House of David. "Virgin" is exactly what the word *virgin* means.

> *Then Joseph being raised from sleep did as the angel of the Lord had bidden him, and took unto him his wife: And knew her not till she had brought forth her firstborn son: and he called his name JESUS.*
>
> Matthew 1:24-25

He is the Pre-Existent One

The only Gospel without a genealogy is Mark because he is describing Jesus as a suffering servant, and one does not worry about the pedigree of a servant. Then we open the Gospel of John. Of the four gospels, John's genealogy of Jesus is the shortest one. In fact, most people don't recognize this genealogy as actually being as such because it is the genealogy of the Pre-Existent One.

> *In the beginning was the Word, and the Word was with God, and the Word was God. The same was in the beginning with God. All things were made by him; and without him was not any thing made that was made.*
>
> John 1:1-3

> *And the Word was made flesh, and dwelt among us, (and we beheld his glory, the glory as of the only begotten of the Father,) full of grace and truth.*
>
> John 1:14

Also, we must remember what the angel Gabriel said to Mary:

And, behold, thou shalt conceive in thy womb, and bring forth a son, and shalt call his name JESUS. He shall be great, and shall be called the Son of the Highest: and the Lord God shall give unto him the throne of his father David: And he shall reign over the house of Jacob for ever; and of his kingdom there shall be no end.

Luke 1:31-33

Did Jesus ever actually sit on David's throne? He couldn't have because it didn't exist at that time. Jeconiah was the last of David's line to sit on the throne, due to the blood curse on the line of Jeconiah (also known as Jehoiachin and Coniah).

Many Christians miss the idea that His destiny is to fulfill the Davidic Covenant. It is an everlasting covenant. When we say, "Thy Kingdom come" in the Lord's Prayer, we are talking about the Millennial Kingdom, which is the fulfillment of the Davidic Covenant. Jesus is not yet on His father David's throne, He is on His Heavenly Father's throne right now; He is yet to take the throne of His father David, which is an earthly throne.

Notice particularly the second part of that of that verse: "And he shall reign over the house of Jacob forever." He will reign for only a thousand years? No, He will reign forever.

Isaiah 9:6 is a verse we often see on Christmas cards. And we need to recognize at Christmas time just what is being celebrated—the kingdom that He is yet to establish on earth.

> *For unto us a child is born, unto us a son is given: and the government shall be upon his shoulder: and his name shall be called Wonderful, Counsellor, The mighty God, The everlasting Father, The Prince of Peace.*
>
> Isaiah 9:6

For unto us a child is born—that is his human side. For unto us a son is given—that is his divine side. The terms are NOT synonymous! Both elements are there explicitly. "A child is born," "a son is given," is very, very key. The first is human, the second is divine.

Isaiah continues:

> *Of the increase of his government and peace there shall be no end, upon the throne of David, and upon his kingdom, to order it, and to establish it with judgment and with justice from henceforth even for ever. The zeal of the LORD of hosts will perform this.*
>
> Isaiah 9:7

The government is not yet on His shoulders, but it will be. Of course, we all recognize some of that "zeal" at the climax in Revelation 19 with the Final Horseman.

> *And I saw heaven opened, and behold a white horse; and he that sat upon him was called Faithful and True, and in righteousness he doth judge and make war.*
>
> Revelation 19:11
>
> *And he was clothed with a vesture dipped in blood: and his name is called The Word of God.*[16]
>
> Revelation 19:13

That blood is not His, it is the blood of His enemies. All of this is described vividly in Isaiah 63: 1-4.

In summary, here are some of the titles and names ascribed to Jesus Christ:

— The Coming One
— The Second Adam
— the Last Adam
— a Prophet like Moses
— a Priest after the order of Melchizedek, not Levi
— a Champion like Joshua
— an Offering like Isaac
— a King like David
— a Wise Counselor above Solomon
— a Beloved, Rejected, Exalted son like Joseph

Chapter 4
An Integrated Design

The Bible is an integrated design of sixty-six books, penned by over forty different individuals over several thousand years and it anticipates in detail every event that happened. The entire family tree of the Messiah is laid down in detail thousands of years before the fact. At the Cross, hundreds of unique specifications were fulfilled. Mel Gibson's popular movie, *The Passion of the Christ*,[17] gives an unfortunate impression that the Cross was a tragedy. No, it was an achievement, and it was planned before the foundation of the world.

The Authentication of Christ

The authentication of Christ in the Septuagint, the Greek translation of the Old Testament, gives over 300 detailed specifications which are fulfilled by His first coming. One of them—the seventy weeks of Daniel (Daniel 9:24-26)—even predicts the exact day He would present himself as the *Meshiach Nagid* (The Messiah the King), riding that donkey into Jerusalem. That event was prophesized five centuries in advance (Zechariah 9:9). Once you know who He is, then the rest of it—the Torah, Daniel, and all the remainder—are validated. Jesus ties it all together with His comments, His actions, and His identity.

From the integrity of the design, you can demonstrate who Jesus Christ really is and prove it beyond doubt. It is an integrated design that transcends time and space. That's the discovery we need to re-affirm every Christmas because it will change one's entire attitude and perspective of the Bible.

That is the epistemology (the study of knowledge, its scope and limits) that we employ as our structure. First, establish the integrity of design, then establish the identity of Jesus Christ, and each will authenticate the other.

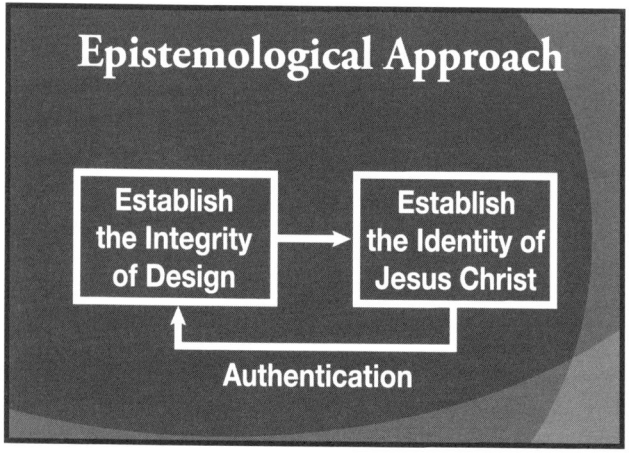

He has the most distinguished family tree in all of history. It's encrypted in the Torah (Genesis 38), prophesied in the Judges (Ruth 4), it evades the blood curse on Jeconiah (Jeremiah 22:30), and results in the virgin birth of Jesus Christ (Genesis 3:15; Isaiah 7:14; Psalm 69; Psalm 110) that we celebrate each year in our holiday season.

Chapter 5
History of the Magi

In order to understand the timing of the birth of Christ, we need some political understanding of the empires as well as the geopolitical landscape of that time. The world's first dictator, Nimrod, built the city of Babylon. The Babylonian Empire rose to power about 606 B.C. The city of Babylon became an empire under the leadership of Nabopolassar's son, a very bright general in his own right, Nebuchadnezzar. Nebuchadnezzar established the Babylonian empire which was eventually absorbed by the Persian Empire when Cyrus the Persian conquered it in 539 B.C. When Cyrus conquered the Babylonians, he was so impressed by the letter Daniel showed him[18] that he encouraged the Jews to return to their land and rebuild their Temple. This return to the land is recorded in the Book of Ezra. The Persian Empire lasted from 539 B.C. to 332 B.C.

Within the Persian Empire there was a group called the Magi. The word *Magi* is a Latinized form of *Magoi*, an ancient Greek transliteration of the original Persian word. Much of our information about the Magi comes from Herodotus, often called The Father of History.[19] As one studies the Magi in Herodotus, their key skill was not astrology, it was dream interpretation (oneiromancy).

Note how similar the Magi were, originally, to the Jewish forms of worship:

— Monotheistic concept of one beneficent creator
— Creator is all-good
— Creator is opposed by all that is evil (malevolent evil spirit)
— Hereditary priesthood:
  Jews had Levites;
  Persians had Magi (therefore, Rab-mag)
— One mediator between God and man
— Made atonement by blood sacrifice
— Same essential concept of clean and unclean
— Depended on divination (wisdom) from the priesthood:
  Levites had Urim and Thummim;
  Magi had *Barsoms* (small bundles of divining rods.)

In the Medo-Persian world, Darius the Great (522 B.C. – 486 B.C.) recognized that the Magi were very, very skilled at dream interpretation. As such, they were attached to the court and they eventually became the king-makers. They are given an interesting title in Jeremiah 39:3,13—*Rab-mag* (the untranslated title of Nergalsharezer, who was the chief of the Magi in Nebuchadnezzar's court).

The Magi were a hereditary priesthood among the Medes. Darius, the King of the Medes, put Daniel (a former Jewish captive) in charge of this hereditary priesthood and bestowed on him the title of Governor (one of three appointed in Daniel 6:2) because Daniel had gained favor with him. One can only imagine how that was received by the "hereditary priesthood." This event, as well as Daniel's refusal to stop praying to his God is probably what led to the plot against Daniel that resulted in the lion's den incident in Daniel 6: 7-28.

As one continues through the history of Persia, one discovers there is a real synergism between Persia and Israel. In fact, in the great Archaemenid days (the first Persian Empire), some of the Persian kings were apparently of Jewish blood.

So, since the days of Daniel, the fortunes of Persia and the Jewish nation are intertwined. They both had their turn falling under the Seleucid Empire in the wake of Alexander's conquests. The Seleucid Empire was a remnant of the Greek Empire. Also, they both were able to get free: the Jews under the Maccabean leadership, and the Persians as the dominating group within the Parthian Empire.

The major rival of Rome to the east was the Parthian Empire. The Parthians had a Council of the Magistanes (which could be the origin of the term *magistrate*). The upper house of that council was composed of men who also held the top governmental offices in the empire. This dual capacity of priest and counselor (magistrate) is where the civil, political, and religious roles became connected in the Persian environment. They became the supreme priestly caste of the Persian Empire—the Magi. Their duties included absolute choice of the king of the realm, and that will impact Herod's reaction when they arrive, seeking "he that is born, King of the Jews"

The Rosetta Stone (a stone block small enough for one to handle) had a vital role in unraveling the Egyptian hieroglyphics. There is another inscription that has essentially the same role: the inscription on Behistun. This is a huge wall, like a billboard, and it was commissioned by Darius the Great. Everything inscribed on it is in three languages: Elamite, Addadian/Babylonian, and the Old Persian or Aramaic. Due to the discovery of that huge wall, we can learn about those languages, and it is the link by which we can translate other languages. The Behistun also speaks of a particular event that has to do with a speedy and final triumph by Darius over a revolt of Magi in 522 B.C.

Alexander the Great

In 331 B.C., Alexander the Great conquered the Persians and made Babylon his capital. He did not destroy Babylon, as many books would suggest. He did however, promote Greek, which is the most precise of languages, as an international standard throughout the region.

After the Persian Empire came the Greek Empire under Alexander the Great, and when Alexander died, four of his generals divided the Empire: Cassandra took the far west, Lysimachus took that area we know as Turkey, Seleucus took the east, and Ptolemy's area was to the south. In time, the two major players were Seleucus and Ptolemy. The map makes it easy to see how that little strip of Israel became a buffer state.

It is the subsequent struggles between these two dynasties that populate the bulk of Daniel 11. Interestingly enough, Daniel 11:5-35 also writes about the so-called "silent years" between the Old and New Testament. His writings about these years are so precise that some critics have said it had to be written later because it really chronicles, in effect, the struggles between Ptolemy's and Seleucus' relative dynasties.

Finally, the Roman Empire (68 B.C.-476 A.D.) succeeded the Greek empire, and the Roman infrastructure was established, which was eventually used for the promotion of the Gospel. The Romans established a common language, Latin, as well as the Roman system of roads, Roman laws, and a unified monetary system.

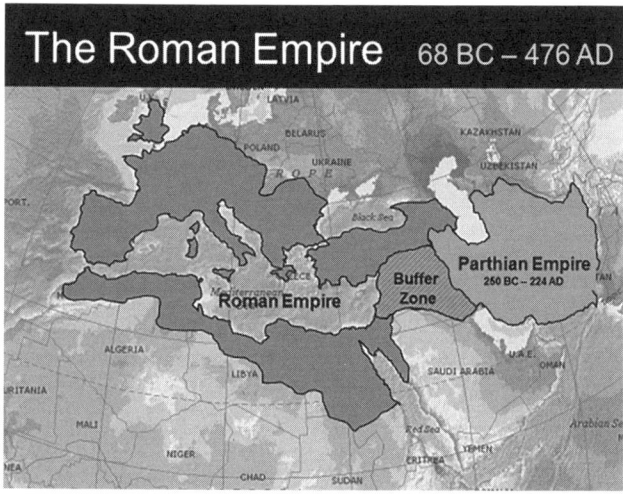

The Roman Empire consisted of two legs, and the eastern leg outlasted the western leg by a thousand years. While Rome was making its mark, the remnants of the Persian Empire, the Parthian Empire, was in its heyday (ca. 250 B.C. to 224 B.C.). The zone that we think of as the Fertile Crescent was really a buffer between the vicissitudes of both empires, Rome and Parthia. The Parthians had succeeded in founding an independent kingdom and during the first century B.C., it grew into an empire extending from the Euphrates River all the way to the Indus River and from the Oxus (now Amu Darya) River to the Indian Ocean.

Parthia, an ancient empire of Asia, was in what are present-day Iran and Afghanistan. The Parthians were of Scythian descent, and they adopted Median dress and Aryan speech. They were subject successively to the Assyrians, Medes, Persians, and Macedonians under Alexander the Great, and then to the Seleucids. In 224 A.D. Parthia was conquered by Ardashir I, King of Persia and founder of the Sassanid dynasty.

The Roman Empire and the Parthians

However, after the middle of the first century B.C., Parthia was a rival of Rome, and several wars occurred between the two powers. Judea is a buffer zone. Parthia had several major successes against Rome when these two powers clashed.

Pompey, the first Roman conqueror of Jerusalem in 63 B.C., attacked the Armenian outpost of Parthia—the western edge of this emerging empire. In 55 B.C., Crassus led the Roman legions in sacking Jerusalem and a subsequent attack on Parthia proper. However, the Romans were decisively defeated at the Battle of Carrhae (53 B.C.), with the loss of 20,000 troops, including their commander.[20] The Parthians counter-attacked with a token invasion of Armenia, Syria, and Palestine. In effect, this places Judea under the Parthian thumb for a while.

Nominal Roman rule was reestablished under Antipater, the father of Herod (who later became King Herod) and yet he had to retreat before a Parthian invasion in 40 B.C. Then Mark Anthony re-established Roman sovereignty in 37 B.C., but like Crassus before him, he embarked on a similarly ill-fated Parthian expedition. His disastrous retreat was followed by another wave of invading Parthians. The Parthian forces swept all Roman opposition completely out of Palestine (including Herod himself who had to flee to Alexandria and then to Rome). With Parthian collaboration, Jewish sovereignty was restored, and Jerusalem was fortified with a Jewish garrison. Palestine was Parthian, not Roman. Rome would claim it, and Herod would finally succeed in receiving the title King of the Jews from the head of the Roman Empire, but for three years, including a five-month siege by Roman troops, King Herod was unable to occupy his own capital city.

Herod had gained the throne of a rebellious buffer-state situated between two mighty, contending empires. He knew that at any time his own subjects might conspire against him and bring the Parthians to their aid. Remember, Herod was not Jewish; he was Idumean, an Edomite, an enemy of the Jews. At the time of the birth of Christ, Herod may have been close to his final illness.

Meanwhile, in Rome, Emperor Augustus was very old by now. Rome, since the retirement of Tiberius, was without any experienced military commander;

a fact that made them concerned about the outlying districts. In addition, pro-Parthian Armenia was fomenting a revolt against Rome, which was successfully accomplished within two years.

Parthia was very powerful, but it had its own problems internally. It was ripe for another invasion to the buffer provinces, except it was racked with internal contention. Phraates IV was a very unpopular and aging king. He had been deposed once before, so it was not improbable that the Persian Magi were already involved in the political maneuvering requisite to choosing his successor. Remember, the Magi had a dual priestly and governmental office; they are essentially like the senior senate of Persia.

The Visit of the Magi

It was a group of Persian-Parthian *king-makers*[21] who entered Jerusalem in the latter days of the reign of Herod. It was conceivable that the Magi could have taken advantage of the king's lack of popularity to further their own interests with the establishment of a new dynasty, if a sufficiently strong contender could be found.[22] This was a very precarious visit for all concerned. And this was not just three guys on camels. These Magi were king-makers. They were accompanied by a major military force, probably a cavalry escort of 1,000 men to insure their safe penetration into Roman territory, and with unimaginable oriental pomp. Scripture records the reaction to their arrival:

> *Now when Jesus was born in Bethlehem of Judaea in the days of Herod the king, behold, there came wise men from the east to Jerusalem, Saying, Where is he that is born King of the Jews? for we have seen his star in the east, and are come to worship him. When Herod the king had heard these things, he was troubled, and all Jerusalem with him.*
>
> Matthew 2:1-3

The whole city of Jerusalem wouldn't be upset about three guys on camels; no, this is a major Parthian group, or entourage, that has arrived, and Herod is nervous. Herod was not really seen as King of the Jews. He was appointed by Rome, and he was also Idumaean. His reaction was understandably one of fear when one considers the background of Roman-Parthian rivalry that prevailed during his lifetime. Their request of Herod, regarding the one "who has been born king of the Jews," was a calculated insult to him because he was someone who had contrived and bribed his way into that office. Herod was paranoid, and that was why he built fortresses like Masada, the Herodian, and ten others. He was troubled because he recognized there was an implied threat in their words.

The first question in the New Testament is, "Where is he that is born King of the Jews?" (Matthew 2:2). The first question by God in the Old Testament is when He called to Adam, "Where art thou?" (Genesis 3:9) The first question in the Old Testament deals with the first Adam; the first question in the New Testament deals with the last Adam.[23]

> *And when he had gathered all the chief priests and scribes of the people together, he demanded of them where Christ should be born. And they said unto him, In Bethlehem of Judaea: for thus it is written by the prophet, And thou Bethlehem, in the land of Juda, art not the least among the princes of Juda: for out of thee shall come a Governor, that shall rule my people Israel.*
>
> Matthew 2:4-6

Matthew is quoting Micah 5:2, which we so often see on Christmas cards:

> *But thou, Bethlehem Ephratah, though thou be little among the thousands of Judah, yet out of thee shall he come forth unto me that is to be ruler in Israel; whose goings forth have been from of old, from everlasting.*
>
> Micah 5:2

This is the pre-eminent One that is going to be born as a man.

We notice that there are two kinds of people found in Matthew 2, those with hatred and those paying homage! The entire world falls into one of these two categories. Also, note that the Magi were Gentiles, not Jews.

> *Then Herod, when he had privily called the wise men, enquired of them diligently what time the*

star appeared. And he sent them to Bethlehem, and said, Go and search diligently for the young child; and when ye have found him, bring me word again, that I may come and worship him also. When they had heard the king, they departed; and, lo, the star, which they saw in the east, went before them, till it came and stood over where the young child was. When they saw the star, they rejoiced with exceeding great joy.

Matthew 2:7-10

The Magi knew about astronomy, but they were looking for something unique, something special, and something which had been prophesied, probably by Daniel. They also knew that He was King of the Jews!

And when they were come into the house, they saw the young child with Mary his mother, and fell down, and worshipped him: and when they had opened their treasures, they presented unto him gifts; gold, and frankincense, and myrrh.

Matthew 2:11

Notice that they are in a house now, and no longer in a stable. This could be a year or more later. Because there are three gifts, most people jump to the conclusion there were three guys. No, it could have been twenty guys or two guys, and there may have been other gifts. However, we do know that there were at least three gifts, and those three are mentioned because they are prophetic.

— Gold speaks of His deity.
— Frankincense was an incense used for priestly duties.[24]
— Myrrh, when crushed, was an ointment for burial.

These gifts speak of His roles as well: King, Priest, and Prophet. In the Millennium, Isaiah 60:6 tell us that He will be given gifts: gold and frankincense (but no myrrh because His death is behind Him.)

> *And being warned of God in a dream that they should not return to Herod, they departed into their own country another way.*
>
> Matthew 2:12

It is important to catch the mention of "a dream" and remember that the Magi were known for their ability to interpret dreams (oneiromancy). God communicated with them in a manner with which they were most comfortable.

Traditions and the Magi

We have looked at what the Scripture says about the birth of Christ, and we have a little bit of a perspective of the geopolitical environment. Now we need to see the incredible traditions that have risen around these Magi.

Numbers and Names

In the Eastern Church, there weren't three, there were twelve Magi, and Christmas is twelve days in length. Their Christmas is January 6, not December 25, but that is just an Eastern Orthodox tradition.

In about the third century, these wise men suddenly become "kings" bearing gifts. This concept probably comes, in part, because of two psalms, although the psalmist was probably referring to the Millennium.

> *Because of thy temple at Jerusalem shall kings bring presents unto thee.*
>
> Psalm 68:29
>
> *The kings of Tarshish and of the isles shall bring presents: the kings of Sheba and Seba shall offer gifts.*
>
> Psalm 72:10

Relics attributed to the Magi were discovered in the fourth century; transferred from Constantinople to Milan in the fifth century, and shipped to Cologne by Frederick Barbarossa in 1162 where they remain enshrined.

The Western tradition, having been influenced by the Reformation and the Medieval Church, places the number of gifts of the Magi at three because of the three Wise Men. And we place Christmas on December 25 for the reasons cited earlier. Some churches, especially Eastern Orthodox, celebrate Epiphany on January 6 and that is twelve days after the birth of Christ, and traditionally when the Wise Men first saw the Christ child, the King of the Jews. Additionally, the Eastern Orthodox tradition will have twelve Magi coming to worship the King of the Jews, Jesus Christ.

In the sixth century, a chronicle, *Exerpia Latina Garbari,* was written and gave the three Wise Men names:

Balthasar (Bithisarea)
Melchoir (Melichior)
Gaspar (Gathaspa)

What derives from this are the three names often used in literature, such as in *Ben Hur*.[25] During the seventh century, these three became representative of Asia, Africa, and Europe by representing the three sons of Noah: Shem, Ham, and Japheth.[26] Of course, this ignores the fact that all "three" wise men were Medes, that is, Gentiles. In the fourteenth century, the Armenians added a slight twist to all of this:

Balthasar was King of Arabia
Melchior was King of Persia
Gaspar was King of India

The Star

Another crucial element surrounding the birth and early life of Christ is the Star. When you go to a planetarium show, especially around Christmas time, they almost always have a program describing various conjunctions and eclipses, and numerous attempts to speculate about the Star of Bethlehem. Some try to tie the Star with Balaam's prophecy. Balaam's prophecy in Numbers 24:17 says there will be a star out of Jacob, but it is interesting that Matthew did not quote that prophecy. There is also Isaiah 60:3 that speaks of "the brightness of your rising."

Astronomers have proposed several theories involving conjunctions. It was Kepler who first suggested the conjunction of Jupiter and Saturn in the constellation of Pisces, which occurred in 7 B.C. This is probably the most popular explanation, but one of the problems with that theory is that the conjunction is about five years too soon.

Those who hold such theories miss the main point—this is not a natural phenomenon. If the star could be proven to be a natural phenomenon, that would destroy its significance. It is significant because it was supernatural. It led them, it moved, and it settled over the spot they had to find.

I suspect something that I have never seen in a commentary.[27] My conjecture is that the Star of Bethlehem was the Shekinah Glory: the observable light that emanates from the manifested presence of God the Holy Spirit in His visible form. This material presence was recorded at the following:

— The Creation, it brooded over the waters (Genesis 1)
— The Abrahamic Covenant, it passed through the split offering (Genesis 25)
— The Burning Bush (Exodus 3)
— The Pillar of fire by night and the Cloud by day (Exodus 13)
— The flames at Pentecost (Acts 2)

So, why wouldn't the same Glory appear here with the Wise Men? Would this not be the same thing? The star was announcing and designating the Messiah. You wonder, what caused the Star of Bethlehem? It was the Holy Spirit in a visible form.[28]

Chapter 6
To Egypt and Nazareth

And when they were departed, behold, the angel of the Lord appeareth to Joseph in a dream, saying, Arise, and take the young child and his mother, and flee into Egypt, and be thou there until I bring thee word: for Herod will seek the young child to destroy him. When he arose, he took the young child and his mother by night, and departed into Egypt: And was there until the death of Herod: that it might be fulfilled which was spoken of the Lord by the prophet, saying, Out of Egypt have I called my son.

Matthew 2:13-15

Matthew is implying that there is a symbolic connection between the history of Christ and the history of Israel. He is pointing out that some of the Old Testament passages that discuss the nation Israel also have a valid Messianic interpretation. Jesus Christ, as a babe, was sent to Egypt for a while, was called out, and later went into the wilderness—just like Israel. Jesus fasted 40 days in the wilderness; Israel was in the wilderness forty years. We also have the Passover Lamb foreshadowed in Egypt by Israel, and fulfilled in Christ, the Passover Lamb of God.

When Israel was a child, then I loved him, and called my son out of Egypt.

Hosea 11:1

This is one of the prophetic references that we need to consider more deeply. Hosea was written some 700 years before the birth of Christ. When we examine this verse in the context of the verses preceding and following, we discover that this passage is about the nation of Israel. Matthew tells us this verse is a Messianic prophecy. Why? Matthew was Jewish, and he understood that pattern is prophecy.

God speaks of the nation of Israel as His son. The first time is in Exodus 4:22. Other references include Jeremiah 31:9 and Romans 9:4-5.

And thou shalt say unto Pharaoh, Thus saith the LORD, Israel is my son, even my firstborn:

Exodus 4:22

They shall come with weeping, and with supplications will I lead them: I will cause them to walk by the rivers of waters in a straight way, wherein they shall not stumble: for I am a father to Israel, and Ephraim is my firstborn.

Jeremiah 31:9

Who are Israelites; to whom pertaineth the adoption, and the glory, and the covenants, and the giving of the law, and the service of God, and the promises; Whose are the fathers, and of whom as concerning the flesh Christ came, who is over all, God blessed for ever. Amen.

Romans 9:4-5

All through the Book of Isaiah, the thought shifts between the nation and the Messiah. In Isaiah 41:8, Israel is spoken of as if the nation was an individual, "But you, Israel, are My servant…." Isaiah 42:1-4 states, "I have put My Spirit upon Him…." The subject has changed and no longer refers to the nation; now it refers to the Messiah.

There is an antiphonal style in Isaiah where it is the nation at one time, the Messiah the next. The Jews understand this, and can see these things as prophetic. That is why they study their history in terms of anticipating the future. Isaiah 52:13 through the next chapter is perhaps the peak of this kind of writing. The Jews interpret Isaiah 53 nationally, not individually. They deny that it refers to the Messiah because it is too much of an indictment of the rejection of the New Testament Christ.

Rabbi Yitzhak Kaduri

Yitzhak Kaduri was one of the most prominent ultra-Orthodox rabbis in Israel. He was so unique and well-respected that when he died at 108 years of age (or even older) over 200,000 people came to his funeral. He died in February 2006.

A few months before he died, he wrote a small note which he requested should remain sealed for a year after his death. This was somewhat of a strange procedure, but we now understand why he requested that it remain sealed.

One year after his death the note was opened and it made the front pages of the national press in Israel.

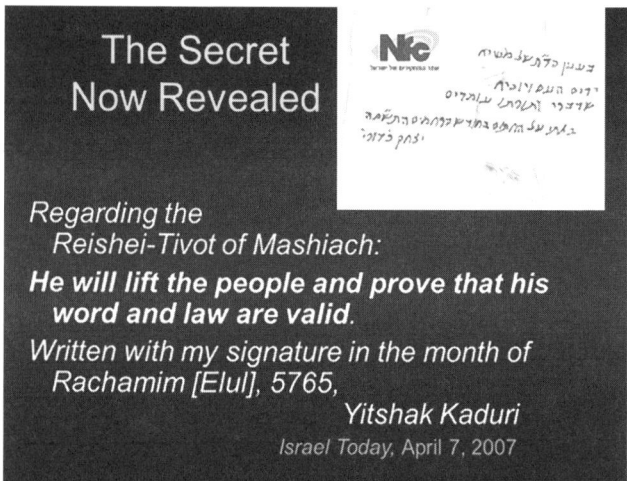

It was April 7, 2007 when this appeared in the paper. What one does not understand unless one is a Kabbalist, as Rabbi Kaduri was, that by taking the first letter of each word in the Hebrew, the result indicates that the name of the Messiah is *Yehoshua*, or *Yeshua*. This has rattled the ultra-orthodox community because they understand what he was doing.

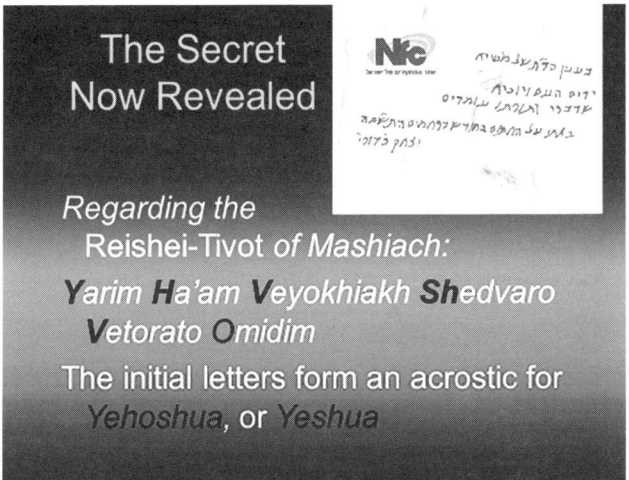

In Judaism, it is considered poor form to speak ill of someone who has been dead for more than a year. After one year, the person has veneration, so he had this note sealed until one year after his death. He knew the bomb it would drop on the ultra-orthodox community because of the legacy he left. Kaduri's legacy was a written document that had a total of eighteen points; it was posted on his disciples' website.[29] Here are a few of the points:

1) The Spirit of the Messiah is the spirit of prophecy.

2) A person is conceived by the Messiah and contains the spirit of Messiah when he meets Messiah

3) True believers in Messiah … draw others to the testimony of Messiah… anyone who will teach and do this will be called great in the kingdom of heaven

4) [In Jewish tradition the suffering Messiah son of Joseph precedes the coming of the victorious Messiah son of David. –*website ed.*] The union of the 2 Messiahs has taken place. Indeed the 2 Messiahs are one, they are one soul.

5) The rabbi was told he would be privileged to see Messiah in his own lifetime, which has indeed taken place, and he was saved.

6) …"The spirit of the Lord will rest on Him." (Isaiah 11:2).

7) By His words He will gather the outcasts of Israel from all over the world. And He will lift up a standard for the nations (Isaiah 11:12).

8) He will strike the earth with the rod of His mouth and with the breath of His lips He will slay the wicked (Isaiah 11:4).

9) By the word of the Lord the heavens were made (Psalm 33:6)[30]

In point fourteen, Kaduri quoted from Isaiah 53 and applies it to the Messiah. This is not a chapter applied to the Messiah by conventional Judaism.

In point sixteen, he indicated that accepting the Messiah "is easier for those who do not keep the Torah." That comment echoes from Isaiah 9:1.

It is possible that this may be the beginning of the blindness being lifted from the nation of Israel that Paul talks about in Romans 11:25.

> *For I would not, brethren, that ye should be ignorant of this mystery, lest ye should be wise in your own conceits; that blindness in part is happened to Israel, until the fulness of the Gentiles be come in.*
>
> Romans 11:25

Understanding all of the above, we will move back to Herod the Great and his role in the infanticide which occurred in Bethlehem and in surrounding areas.

Herod and the Babies of Bethlehem

> *Then Herod, when he saw that he was mocked of the wise men, was exceeding wroth, and sent forth, and slew all the children that were in Bethlehem, and in all the coasts thereof, from two years old and under, according to the time which he had diligently enquired of the wise men. Then was fulfilled that which was spoken by Jeremy the prophet, saying, In Rama was there a voice heard, lamentation, and weeping, and great mourning, Rachel weeping for her children, and would not be comforted, because they are not.*
>
> Matthew 2:16-18

Apparently the wise men could have arrived a substantial period after the actual birth of Christ or maybe it was within a year and Herod added a year to be on the safe side. It's a matter of speculation.

Matthew sees the butchering, the massacre in Bethlehem, as the fulfillment of Jeremiah's prophecy:

> *Thus saith the LORD; A voice was heard in Ramah, lamentation, and bitter weeping; Rahel weeping for her children refused to be comforted for her children, because they were not.*
>
> Jeremiah 31:15

Rachel is being used by Jeremiah, idiomatically, as "mother Israel." A rabbinical mind would notice this idiom and begin to look for a pattern that might be repeated in the future—a prophecy. As she died in labor, she called the son *Ben-o-ni*, "son or my sorrow, or travail." Jacob renamed him Benjamin, "Son of my right hand." This is a pattern that we find applied to Messiah. Isaiah 53 calls Messiah "a man of sorrows" and Psalm 2 refers to Him as the "Son of my right hand." Remember, to the Jewish mind, prophecy is also pattern.

> *But when Herod was dead, behold, an angel of the Lord appeareth in a dream to Joseph in Egypt, Saying, Arise, and take the young child and his mother, and go into the land of Israel: for they are dead which sought the young child's life. And he arose, and took the young child and his mother, and came into the land of Israel. But when he*

> *heard that Archelaus did reign in Judaea in the room of his father Herod, he was afraid to go thither: notwithstanding, being warned of God in a dream, he turned aside into the parts of Galilee: And he came and dwelt in a city called Nazareth: that it might be fulfilled which was spoken by the prophets, He shall be called a Nazarene.*
>
> Matthew 2:19-23

Evidently Joseph settled up north and not in Judea. So He is called a Nazarene. That term actually implies, in the common vernacular, an ignorant man. And, it's partly because it was virtually a Gentile area up in the north. It was a figure of speech which implied contempt. However, this passage does imply that they went to Nazareth after Egypt, not before. Nazareth was not the place where the wise men came to worship the child.

The Branch

> *And there shall come forth a rod out of the stem of Jesse, and a Branch shall grow out of his roots:*
>
> Isaiah 11:1

The Hebrew word used here for Branch is *netzer* – a sprout that grows out from a stump. It has been suggested that these are intended puns. A pun is a deliberate connotative transfer, usually intended for humor. The Holy Spirit uses puns all through the Scripture. Jeremiah 33:15, Zechariah 6:12 and elsewhere have examples of this.

One of these idioms is *tsemach,* which is translated "a branch." Here are some examples of this word being used idiomatically for Christ:

> *In that day shall the branch of the LORD be beautiful and glorious, and the fruit of the earth shall be excellent and comely for them that are escaped of Israel.*
>
> Isaiah 4:2

> *Behold, the days come, saith the LORD, that I will raise unto David a righteous Branch, and a King shall reign and prosper, and shall execute judgment and justice in the earth.*
>
> Jeremiah 23:5

> *In those days, and at that time, will I cause the Branch of righteousness to grow up unto David; and he shall execute judgment and righteousness in the land.*
>
> Jeremiah 33:15

> *Hear now, O Joshua the high priest, thou, and thy fellows that sit before thee: for they are men wondered at: for, behold, I will bring forth my servant the BRANCH.*
>
> Zechariah 3:8

> *And speak unto him, saying, Thus speaketh the LORD of hosts, saying, Behold the man whose name is The BRANCH; and he shall grow up out of his place, and he shall build the temple of the LORD:*
>
> Zechariah 6:12

Chapter 7
The Mazzaroth and the Zodiac

We all know the name of some of the stars and star clusters: the North Star, the Seven Sisters, the Big Dipper, the Little Dipper, Orion, and others. Psalm 147 and Isaiah tells us that all the stars have a name:

He telleth the number of the stars; he calleth them all by their names.

Psalm 147:4

Lift up your eyes on high, and behold who hath created these things, that bringeth out their host by number: he calleth them all by names by the greatness of his might, for that he is strong in power; not one faileth.

Isaiah 40:26

The number of stars in the heavens is beyond our imagining; beyond our ability to really represent them numerically. Yet they each have a name, and God calls them by name.

We are familiar with the Zodiac, and its twelve signs. We call the astrological calendar the Zodiac because we follow the Babylonian tradition, but in the Hebrew tradition it is called the Mazzaroth. The word Zodiac that we use comes from Sodi, "the way." That is also what the Christian path was called in the Book of Acts. That is what the "signs in the heavens" were originally called because they illustrated a message. Most of our information, the oldest information we have from secular sources, is from the Temple of Denderah, circa 2000 B.C. or about 4,000 years ago. But that is the secular picture. Psalm 19, we must remind ourselves states:

> *The heavens declare the glory of God; and the firmament sheweth his handywork. Day unto day uttereth speech, and night unto night sheweth knowledge. There is no speech nor language, where their voice is not heard. Their line is gone out through all the earth, and their words to the end of the world. In them hath he set a tabernacle for the sun, Which is as a bridegroom coming out of his chamber, and rejoiceth as a strong man to run a race. His going forth is from the end of the heaven, and his circuit unto the ends of it: and there is nothing hid from the heat thereof.*
>
> Psalm 19:1-6

People will often say that is obviously archaic because we know the sun doesn't go around the earth. In fact, that is not what it says. It says the sun goes from one end of heaven to the other. The fact that we are going around our whole Galaxy every twenty-five thousand years is missed by them unless they have had some astronomy.

If one is familiar with the Mazzaroth, one knows that there are twelve signs, just like in our Zodiac. However, in the Mazzaroth, the twelve signs spell out the plan of God from the virgin birth to the triumph of the Lion of the tribe of Judah, if one knows the names in Hebrew.

Each of the twelve signs of the Mazzaroth is associated with one of the twelve tribes of Israel. The first sign in our vernacular is called Virgo, or the Virgin. It is associated with the tribe of Zebulun, where Nazareth is located.

If you know the names of the stars, in their order of brightness, by their Hebrew names, it spells out a story. The picture is to remind you of the story. It is the meaning of the story that is important; it's not necessarily what the stars look like. It's the story that counts.

The major Mazzaroth sign we want to study is Virgo, the Virgin. Alpha, the brightest star in the constellation, is Spica (in Latin), which means "an ear of corn." The Hebrew name is *Tsemach*, "the branch." The name in Arabic is *Al Zimach,* "branch" and in Egyptian, it is *Aspolia,* "the seed." The virgin has a branch in her right hand and an ear of corn in her left hand. *Zerah* also means "the seed," and in Genesis 3 we read about "the seed of the woman."

> *Now to Abraham and his seed were the promises made. He saith not, And to seeds, as of many; but as of one, And to thy seed, which is Christ.*
> Galatians 3:16

Jesus explains in John 12:16, "…except a corn of wheat fall into the ground and die, it abideth alone: but if it die, it bringeth forth much fruit."

Tsemach is the branch, and it speaks of the dual nature: He is God and yet He is despised. The double nature is hinted at in the mythology surrounding the constellation. The double nature is embedded in the idea of the sin offering of the despised one, who, at the same time is a ruling King. In 1893, it was discovered that Tsemach is a double star.[31]

Chapter 8
Egypt and Ethiopia

At this point, we need to travel to Egypt and Ethiopia for some background on eschatology, oddly enough. There is a documented tradition that the Ark of the Covenant went to Elephantine Island in 642 B.C., and then to Tana Qirgos Island in Lake Tana, where it remained for about 800 years. There is also archaeological evidence that the tabernacle was set up there from 525 B.C. to 404 B.C.

From there it went to Axum where it is presently at St. Mary's Zion Church. The people there believe it is their commitment to present this Ark to the Messiah when He rules on Mount Zion:

> *From beyond the rivers of Ethiopia my suppliants, even the daughter of my dispersed, shall bring mine offering.*
>
> Zephaniah 3:10

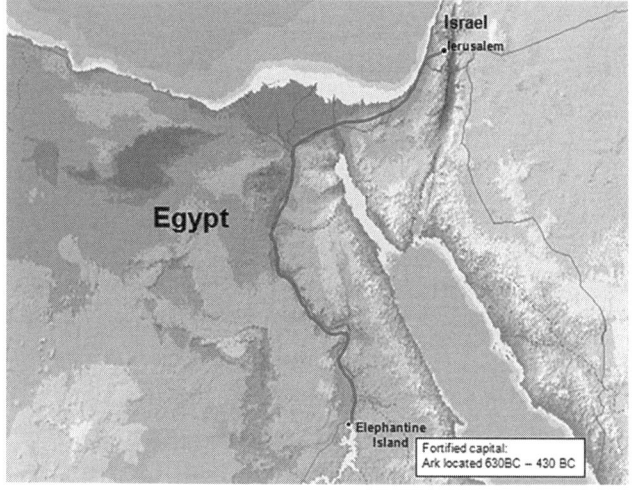

A group of us were fortunate enough to actually go to Elephantine Island, which was the capitol of Egypt in the days when the Levites carried the Ark of the Covenant from Jerusalem. They fled for refuge under Pharaoh Necho, who was Pharaoh of Egypt, but he actually was Ethiopian. In our visit to this island, we saw the place where they stored their artifacts, and we also saw the places where apparently they actually set up the tabernacle for a time.

Elephantine Island

- Early advance outpost of Egypt
  - Southernmost border town
  - Fortified installation serving as First Dynasty fortress
  - Military importance during XXV Dynasty

- Temple to YHWH served Jewish colony prior to Persian occupations of 525-404 BC

>   Elephantine, Official Guidebook,
>   German Institute of Archaeology,
>   Cairo, 1998

The reason to discuss this is because the people there showed us their "bible." In their "bible," they record the visit of Joseph and Mary and the infant baby during the time they had to sojourn in Egypt when fleeing Herod. Their claim is that the family visited Tana Qirgos at that time.

The Young Years of Christ

As we move from the birth of Christ into his young years, there is a final prophecy that Jacob gave in Genesis 49:

The scepter shall not depart from Judah, nor a lawgiver from between his feet, until Shiloh[32] (He whose right it is) and unto him shall the gathering of the people be.

Genesis 49:10

It is a Messianic passage that implies the scepter shall not depart from Judah. The "scepter" refers to the tribal identity and the right to apply Mosaic Laws. Even when the Jews were in captivity in Babylon for seventy years (606-537 B.C.), they were allowed to retain their tribal identity. They had their own logistics and judges (Ezekiel 1:5, 8). The proper translation would then be: "the scepter will not depart from Judah until He comes to whom it belongs." The early Rabbis and Talmudic authorities all through the rabbinical literature understood the meaning.

After Herod the Great died in 6-7 A.D., Archelaus, the second son of Herod the Great, was appointed "Entharch" by Caesar Augustus. However, Archelaus was badly rejected, dethroned and banished, according to Josephus.[33] Herod's first son, Herod Antipater, had been murdered by Herod the Great, along with other family members.[34] Caponius was appointed Procurator at that time. The legal power of the Sanhedrin was immediately restricted, and the adjudication of capital cases *(jus gladii)* was lost. This was normal Roman policy.[35]

The Scepter has Departed from Judah

After the death of Procurator Porcius Festus (61-62 A.D.), after only two years in office, Emperor Nero appointed Albinius to be Procurator in Israel. About the time he succeeded Festus, the high priest Ananias considered it a favorable opportunity to assemble the Sanhedrin. He caused James, the half-brother of Jesus, who was called Christ, and several others to appear before this hastily assembled council, and pronounced upon them the sentence of death by stoning.

All the wise men and strict observers of the law who were at Jerusalem expressed their disapprobation of this act, as recorded in *Antiquities* 20:9 by Josephus and Cf *Jerusalem Talmud*, Sanhedrin, folio 24. Josephus continues by stating that some even went to Albinus himself, who had departed to Alexandria, to bring this breach of the law under his observation and to inform him that Aranius had acted illegally in assembling the Sanhedrin without Roman authority. In effect, Rome had taken away the authority of the Sanhedrin to issue or carry out a death sentence.

All of this was important because the Sanhedrin no longer had the right of adjudication for capital crimes, and they interpreted losing this right as "the scepter departs." So the priests did something very interesting. The Babylonian Talmud records this: they put on sackcloth and ashes, officially mourned, and marched around the city saying, "Woe unto us for the scepter has departed from Judah and the Messiah has not come!"[36] They actually believed that the Word of God had been broken, or failed, and they mourned that fact.

They were unaware that while they were mourning, there was a young boy in a carpenter's shop in Nazareth learning a trade from his earthly father, Joseph. That young man would present Himself as the Messiah the King on the very day that had been predicted by the Angel Gabriel five centuries earlier (Daniel 9:25ff). So Messiah had come.[37]

Review of Major Lessons

A lot of detail has been covered thus far, and there is always a danger of losing the "forest through the trees" in such cases. So here is a short review of the "forest."

The Messianic Line: The truth is in the details. We learn that God always rewards the diligent student who will thoroughly explore a topic. Digging deeper often reveals a treasure we had no idea was there.

The Precision of the God-breathed Text: "All Scripture is given by inspiration of God" (2 Timothy 3:16). The word in the Greek used here for *inspiration* literally means "God-breathed." His Text is precise, and that's why it has so much to offer.

Hermeneutics: This is the theory of interpretation and we must understand that to the Jewish mind, pattern is also prophecy. We need to understand God's patterns.

Psalm 69: The Silent Years in the Life of Christ

It was a surprise to this author to discover that Christ's childhood is recorded in the Word of God.

The Book of Psalms is the most quoted book in the New Testament. Jesus said that the Psalms spoke about Him:

> *And he said unto them, These are the words which I spake unto you, while I was yet with you, that all things must be fulfilled, which were written in the law of Moses, and in the prophets, and in the psalms, concerning me.*
>
> Luke 24:44

> *Then said I, Lo, I come: in the volume of the book it is written of me,*
>
> Psalm 40:7

It turns out that there are many Psalms which constitute irrefutable testimony to the Divine inspiration of the Scriptures in many ways (Psalm 2, 8, 16, 22, 23, 24, 40, 41, 45, 68, 69, 87, 89, 102, 110, 118, etc.). Christ's birth, betrayal, agony, death, resurrection, ascension, coming again in glory, and His worldwide reign are all vividly pictured in the Psalms.

We are going to focus on one Psalm that has an important nuance.[38] Next to Psalm 22, it is the most quoted Psalm in the New Testament. Psalm 22 deals with the death of Christ and Psalm 69 deals with the life of Christ.

Psalm 69 is quoted in the Gospels of Matthew, Mark, Luke, John, and in Acts and Romans. There are also many references to it other than direct quotes. In Psalm 69 there is an allusion to the early years. This Psalm gives us a glimpse into "the silent years," as they are often called, of Christ's childhood and his young manhood of which the Gospels tell us practically nothing.

Dr. Luke records an incident in the life of our Lord when He was twelve years old and in the Temple (Luke 2:41-49). Other than that, we know very little about his childhood. This Psalm fills in some details. We will gain insight into some of His dark days in Nazareth and His dark hours on the cross in this Psalm. This Psalm is classified as an *imprecatory* psalm because of the imprecatory prayer in it (Psalm 69:22-28). It is from that section that most of the New Testament quotes are taken. His cry for justice is a psalm of early humiliation and rejection.

We begin in the north of Israel, in Nazareth. We hear the heart sob of a small boy, a teenager, and a young man.

> *Let not them that wait on thee, O Lord GOD of hosts, be ashamed for my sake: let not those that*

seek thee be confounded for my sake, O God of Israel. Because for thy sake I have borne reproach; shame hath covered my face. I am become a stranger unto my brethren, and an alien unto my mother's children.

Psalm 69:6-8

There are two reasons He was bearing this:

1) They hated Him because of who He was—in the same way the sinner hates the righteous person today.

2) He came to take a lowly, humble place on earth—He bore reproach, and shame covered His face. Verse eight is a strange verse: "I am become a stranger unto my brethren, and an alien unto my mother's children"—not His father's children because Joseph was not His blood father; His siblings were half-brothers and half-sisters. They may have taunted Him and it could have been an unhappy home for Jesus.

This verse also teaches the virgin birth of Christ. A very strange phrase for the psalmist to use is "… and an alien unto my mother's children". Whenever one sees an apparently unnecessary detail, there is a need to look at it more closely. That is what the rabbis will call a *remez*, a hint of something deeper. It's like a sign that says, "Dig here." It is possible that Mary's other boys, James, Judas and Joses said something like, "Mother, we heard someone say that Jesus is not really our brother. They said that nobody knows who His real father is."[39] His apparent illegitimacy may have been a common buzz about Him and His mother. Mary had other children; we know that from the Gospels.

Is not this the carpenter's son? Is not his mother called Mary? And his brethren, James, and Joses, Judas and Simon? And are not his sisters here with us?

Mark 6:3

Four brothers are named here: James, Joses, Simon, and Judas, so there were at least four half-brothers. James and Jude later become believers, and they each wrote a book of the New Testament. We know He had four brothers and at least two sisters; it was apparently a family of seven children, maybe more. Jesus was apparently viewed as having taken up Joseph's trade as a "carpenter." (Hebrew: *charash*; Greek: *tekton*).[40]

The Psalmist continues:

For the zeal of thine house hath eaten me up; and the reproaches of them that reproached thee are fallen upon me.

Psalm 69:9

That verse is quoted in the New Testament when He cleared the Temple:

And found in the temple those that sold oxen and sheep and doves, and the changers of money sitting. And when he had made a scourge of small cords, he drove them all out of the temple, and the sheep, and the oxen; and poured out the changers' money, and overthrew the tables. And said unto them that sold doves, take these things hence; make not my Father's house a house of merchandise. And his disciples remembered that it was written, 'the zeal of thine house has eaten me up.'"

John 2:14-17

The disciples link that to Psalm 69. They were well aware of Psalm 69. The Greek word for *zeal* signifies "to stretch out the neck," a metaphor from the racers who strain every limb to reach forward to lay hold of the prize.

And as we continue in Psalm 69:

When I wept, and chastened my soul with fasting, that was to my reproach.

Psalm 69:10

When He would fast or weep, His brothers would ridicule Him for it. They would probably assume that He was just putting on an act. When He (Jesus) was pious they made fun of Him.

I made sackcloth also my garment; and I became a proverb to them.

Psalm 69:11

The word circulated around that He was illegitimate. In John 8: 41b-48, when He is tangling with the Pharisees, and they say, "We were not born of fornication…." They threw His apparent illegitimacy in His face. In John 8, before that chapter finishes,

He tells them about their parentage in no uncertain terms in John 8:

> *You are of your father the devil, and the desires of your father you want to do.*
>
> John 8:44

> *They that sit in the gate speak against me; and I was the song of the drunkards*
>
> Psalm 69:12

Those who "sit in the gate" are the high officials of the town, the judges. The best people in Nazareth also spoke against Him. The drunks of the town are making up little unkind songs in the tavern about Him and His mother. We all know how unforgiving small towns are. His life in Nazareth could not have been nice.

Why did He endure all of this? He was reared in a town where He was called illegitimate—why? We really have no idea what He went through for those thirty years prior to His ministry. What we do know is that He was faithful in all things so that we might become a legitimate son or daughter of God. The Son of God bore insult, injury, and indignation for each of us, reaching its apex at the Crucifixion. He paid the ultimate penalty for our sins and ensured our adoption as children of God for eternity.

Egypt and Ethiopia

Our Coming King
(Inspired by Pastor S.D. Lockridge)

- He is:
  - King of the Jews (*racial*);
  - King of Israel *(national);*
  - King of all the Ages;
  - King of Heaven;
  - King of Glory;
  - King of Kings…and Lord of Lords.

> ***Do you know Him?***
> ***Do you** really?*

We often forget that He is Jewish. When we celebrate His birth, we need to realize that He was born Jewish. And, the real question this, and every, Christmas season: Do you know Him? Do you <u>really</u> know Him?

> A prophet before Moses;
> A priest after Melchizedek;
> A champion like Joshua;
> An offering in place of Isaac;
> A king from the line of David;
> A wise counselor above Solomon;
> A beloved—rejected—exalted son like
>   Joseph.
>> *And yet far more…*

The Heavens declare His glory…
And the firmament shows His handiwork…
> He who *is,*
> who *was,*
> and who always will be;

The first and the last
> He is the **Alpha** and **Omega**
> The **Aleph** and the **Tau**
> The **A** and the **Z**

He is the first fruits of them that slept.
- He is the *eg-o'i-mee'*
  the *haw-yah' ash-er' hay-yah'*
  The "**I AM that I AM**"
  > *The voice of the Burning Bush!*
  - the Captain of the Lord's Host
  - the conqueror of Jericho

- He is enduringly strong;
  - entirely sincere;
  - eternally steadfast;

- He is immortally graceful;
  - Imperially powerful;
  - Impartially merciful;

> In Him dwells
> The fullness of the Godhead bodily;
> The very God of very God.

> He is our Kinsman-Redeemer
> And He is our Avenger of Blood;
> He is our City of Refuge;

> Our performing High Priest,
> Our Personal Prophet,
> Our Reigning King.

- He's the loftiest idea in Literature;
- He's the highest personality in Philosophy;
- He's the fundamental doctrine of Theology;
- He's the Supreme Problem in "higher criticism"!
- He's the Miracle of the Ages;
  - The superlative of everything good!

We are the beneficiaries of
A Love Letter:

It was **written in blood,**
  on a **wooden cross**
    erected in Judea
      2,000 years ago.

He was crucified on a cross of wood
  Yet He made the hill
  On which it stood.

By Him were all things made
  That were made;
    Without Him was not anything made
      That was made;
By Him are all things held together!

What held Him to that cross?
  It wasn't the nails!
(At any time He could have declared,
  "I'm out of here!")
  It was His love for you and me.

He was born of a woman
   so that we could be born of God;
He humbled Himself
   so that we could be lifted up;
He became a servant
   so that we could be made co-heirs;
He suffered rejection
   so that we could become His friends;
He denied Himself
   so that we could freely receive all things;
He gave Himself
   so that He could bless us in every way.

*He is **available** to the **tempted** and the **tried**;*
*He **blesses** the **young**;*
*He **cleanses** the **lepers**;*
*He **defends** the **feeble**;*
*He **delivers** the **captives**;*
*He **discharges** the **debtors**;*
*He **forgives** the **sinners**;*
*He **franchises** the **meek**;*
*He **guards** the **besieged**;*
*He **heals** the **sick**;*
*He **provides strength** to the **weak**;*
*He **regards** the **aged**;*
*He **rewards** the **diligent**;*
*He **serves** the **unfortunate**;*
*He **sympathizes** and He **saves**!*

His **Offices** are manifold;
His **Reign** is righteous;
His **Promises** are sure;
His **Goodness** is limitless;
His **Light** is matchless;
His **Grace** is sufficient;
His **Love** never changes;
His **Mercy** is everlasting;
His **Word** is enough;
His **Yoke** is easy, and
His **Burden** is light!

- *He's indescribable;*
- *He's incomprehensible;*
- *He's irresistible;*
- **He's invincible!**

The Heaven of heavens
   cannot contain Him;
      Man cannot explain Him

The Pharisees couldn't stand Him
   and learned that they couldn't stop Him;

Pilate couldn't find any fault in Him;
   the witnesses couldn't agree against Him.

Herod couldn't kill Him
   death couldn't handle Him
      the grave couldn't hold Him!

He has always been and always will be;

He had no predecessor and
   will have no successor;

You can't impeach Him and
   He isn't going to resign!

His name is above every name;
   That at the name of **Yeshua**

**Every knee shall bow,
every tongue shall confess**
That ***Jesus Christ is Lord!***
His is the kingdom, the power,
   and the glory…for ever, and ever

…AMEN!

Endnotes

1. See *Tertullian Adversus Judaeos*

2. See Eusebius, *Ecclesiastical History, Book 1, Chapter 5*

3. According to some scholars, the Hebrew word for pregnancy has a gematria of 271. That would make the birth date of Christ on September 20, 2 B.C.

4. The winter solstice is typically around December 22 on our calendar, and the summer solstice is about June 20, 21, or 22. Saturnalia was the worship of the sun.

5. See Isaiah 13 and 14, Jeremiah 50 and 51, and Revelation 18:3

6. The Legend of Tammuz states that Nimrod was considered a "god" and was represented as "The Great Tree." The "Yule Log" would be the "infant" from that tree. So, the "infant" (Tammuz) would die on the day of the Winter Solstice and be reincarnated the next day as Nimrod. Queen Semiramis was the major force behind this celebration and Semiramis was the original name for Thyatira, the recipient of the fourth letter to the seven churches in Revelation (Rev. 2:18-29).

7. "Long Day of Joshua." *Signs in the Heavens*, Chapter 2. Koinonia House Topical Study, CDA35.

8. The issue was not about determining the date of the crucifixion, it was about the day and manner of observing the Paschal Fast. The word, quartodecimens, means 14th and the Biblical law clearly commands one specific day as the day of the Passover sacrifice: the fourteenth of Nisan (Abib). (Lev. 23:32) The history of the early church indicates how anti-Semitic it was and how those trying to be Biblical were actually disdained by the official organizations.

9 The Greek and Hebrew languages are distinctive in that each letter of the alphabet has a numerical value. In Greek, a couple have been abandoned through the years, but it has that same characteristic. That means that every word has a numerical value. Also, every verb in the Greek language has to meet five independent conditions to fit in properly.

10 See Deut. 25:9-10 to understand Ruth 4:7-8. This business with the shoe was an old custom.

11 Normal procedure here, where the call to a Levirate marriage was taking place, would be for the would-be bride to confront the near kinsman. Boaz takes that responsibility and confronts the man himself (Ruth 4:1-10).

12 Numbers 26:33; 27:1-11; 36:2-12; Joshua 17:3-6; 1 Chronicles 7:15

13 Ezra 2:61; Nehemiah 7:63; Numbers 32:41, cf. 1 Chronicles 2:21-22, 34-35; Numbers 27:3-8

14 Salathiel, the ("adopted") son of Jeconiah (Mt 1:12; 1 Ch 3:17) is also called the son of Neri (Lu 3:27). If these are the same person, a probable explanation is that the son of Neri, the descendant of Nathan, was deemed heir to the throne of David on the death of Jeconiah (Jer. 22:30) due to the blood curse. From E. W. Bullinger's *Companion Bible*, App 99.

15 Immanuel means "God with us."

16 See also John 1:1 to define Jesus as the Word of God.

17 *The Passion of the Christ*. Icon Productions: Beverly Hills, CA, 2004. Film.

18 See Isaiah 45 for the letter that Cyrus read. A letter that was addressed to him by name.

19 Herodotus, 1:101. Herodotus was a Greek historian, born at Halicarnassus in Asia Minor (Turkey) in ca.484 B.C. He was born a Persian subject, but immigrated to Greece at a young age.

20 Crassus marched into Parthia with seven legions, nearly four thousand horsemen and as many light-armed troops. Twenty thousand were said to have died and ten thousand taken prisoner. It was the worst Roman defeat since the disastrous loss to Hannibal at Cannae in 216 B.C. Source: penelope.uchicago.edu/~/encyclopaedia_romana/miscellanea/trivia/carrhae.html

21 The Magi, in their dual priestly and governmental office, made up the upper house of the council of the Magistanes (magistrates). Included in their duties was the absolute choice and election of the king of the realm.

22 Within two years Phraataces, the parricide son of Phraates IV, was duly installed by the Magi as the new ruler of Parthia. Later, Philo of Alexandria, Cicero, and others record that Magi were attached to senior Roman courts with acknowledged gifts and standing.

23 See 1 Corinthians 15:45 for Paul's reference to the "first Adam" and the "last Adam."

24 Frankincense was usually mixed with the Temple showbread by the priests

25 Wallace, Lewis. *Ben-Hur : A Tale of the Christ*. Authorized ed. Leipzig: Tauchnitz, 1888.

26 The Venerable Bede (673-735)

27 Dr. Chuck Missler was a member of the Los Angeles Astronomical Society, and made astronomy his hobby for many years.

28 See *Signs in the Heavens* for a discussion of the Hebrew Mazzaroth and the Zodiac. Koinonia House, Coeur d'Alene, ID.

29 http://tulisanmurtad.blogspot.com/2012/07/rabbi-kaduri-reveals-name-of-messiah.html

30 This is an allusion to His divinity, and a non-accepted tenet in Judaism. This is probably the most interesting verse because Kaduri is alluding to the Messiah as divine, as the Creator, and a Jewish rabbi would not normally be comfortable with the idea that Messiah is God.

31 See Signs in the Heavens for a discussion of the Hebrew Mazzaroth and the Zodiac. Koinonia House, Coeur d'Alene, ID.

32 The term Shiloh was understood by the early rabbis and Talmudic authorities as referring to the Messiah. This is according to *Targum Onkelos, Targum Jonathan, and Targum Yerusahlmi.*

33 Flavius Josephus, *Antiquities*, 17:13

34 The joke in the Roman court by Caesar Augustus himself was that one was safer being Herod's pig than Herod's son. In view of such executions, the emperor Augustus reportedly quipped, "It is better to be Herod's pig than son" (Macrobius, *Saturnalia*, 2:4:11)—the joke being that, since Herod was a Jew, he didn't eat pork and his pig would be safe.

35 Flavius Josephus, *Wars of the Jews,* 2:8; also, T*he Jerusalem Talmud,* Sanhedrin, folio 24.

36 *Babylonian Talmud,* Chapter 4, folio 37; also, Augustin Lemann, *Jesus before the Sanhedrin,* 1886, translated by Julius Magath, NL#239683, Library of Congress #15-24873.

37 *The Messiah: An Aramaic Interpretation; The Messianic Exegesis of the Targum*, Samson H. Levy, Hebrew Union College Jewish Institute of Religion, Cincinnati, 1974.

38 Author's note: This is a nuance in Psalm 69 that I have missed in the past.

39 Author's note: It must have been interesting when they later discover who He really is!

40 Hebrew: *charash*; Greek: *texton*: This word, which is a general word for graver or craftsman, is translated "carpenter" in 2 Kings 22:6; 2 Chronicles 24:12; Ezra 3:7; Isaiah 41:7. The same word is rendered "craftsman" in the American Standard Revision Version of Jeremiah 24:2 and 29:2 and "smith" in the American Standard Revised Version of Zechariah 1:20. In 2 Samuel 5:11; 2 Kings 12:11; 1 Chronicles 14:1; and Isaiah 44:13, Hebrew *charash" occurs with Hebrew ets* (wood) and is more exactly translated "carpenter" or "worker in wood." The Greek Tekton, the corresponding Greek word for Artificer, is translated "carpenter" in Matthew 13:55 and Mark 6:3.

KOINONIA INSTITUTE

"Turning believers into Bereans"

You are invited to undertake a lifelong adventure, exploring the Word of God among an international fellowship without borders — neither intellectual nor geographic.

This is an opportunity to "bloom where you are planted" by studying the Bible — and related topics — in virtual classrooms on the Internet, while discovering the unique calling on your own life and preparing for the challenges which will inevitably emerge on your personal horizon.

To learn more, please visit us at

www.KoinoniaInstitute.org

Koinonia Institute is an online Bible Institute with a focus on verse-by-verse study where serious Christians can grow in knowledge, understanding, awareness and commitment!

Here at KI, we delve into the relevance and reliability of Scripture, including prophetic insight both past and present.

"She got there. That was what she wanted. A book influenced her. Did she tell you that?"

"A lot of people told me that."

"Mother's whole life was changed by that book, about how Californians were buried."

"It was Americans, not just Californians."

"Americans. Mother didn't think it was fair that undertakers should make the rules about how persons were buried."

"Well, my God, who said anything about fair? But Christ Almighty, her ideas were a lot worse. Who could put up with thirty-foot platforms all over the country with dead bodies stretched out on them?"

"The Indians could."

"Not *her* Indians. The Sobobas never went in for anything like that."

"She was a half-breed. She didn't have to be tied down by what any one tribe did. All Indians were being discriminated against, she thought."

"Nobody's going to dispute that. If your poor mother were alive today, she could have people organized and burning down mortuaries so that Indians could have platform burial again. My God, they're tearing down whole universities now for less. Soul food and Swahili! Jesus, how do *they* stack up alongside something important like how your ancestors were buried?"

"Mother would never have done anything like that. Organized or torn down or burned down. She wouldn't even protest. She was shy. She was born to endure. She was afraid to go to your office that day without me."

"What good could you do her? You were nothing but a kid."

"I was Father's daughter. And I was white. And she thought I was smart. I know now that's what she thought. She saved every one of my report cards and every composition I ever wrote."

"You probably were smart. Probably *are*. You're Gene's daughter."

"I'm Mother's, too."

"She was plenty smart in her way. Except for that idea of hers that a lawyer would be able to fix it up so she could be on a platform and be eaten by buzzards instead of worms when she died."

"I would prefer it myself. Wouldn't you?"

"After I'm dead, I don't care what eats me."

"She cared."

"What did your father think of all this?"

"He didn't say. Nothing, I suspect. He lived his life and she could live hers."

"Up a tree was okay with him?"
"I never heard him say it wasn't."
"What did he say when she had that platform built?"
"Nothing. It was for bird watching."
"Buzzard watching."
"They're birds. She watched them. So did I."
"Did your father ever climb up to that platform?"
"Not that I know of."
"He must've once."
"You believe that?"
"It's nothing I want to believe."

Mr. Fosdick put his glasses back on, began to cry, and had to take them off. "I don't want to believe it. Gene was my friend. I'd a thousand times rather be where your mother is than where Gene is."

I watched Mr. Fosdick polish his glasses.

"Eugenia," he said, "you are one-hundred-per-cent Indian. Here your mother's dead, your father's in jail accused of her murder, and I'm the one doing the crying."

"I never was encouraged much to cry when I was young. Mother didn't believe in it, and Father was never around to notice. I'm sorry Mother's dead. But being in jail doesn't mean you're guilty."

"You don't get there without damned strong evidence that you belong there."

"They haven't much evidence against Father."

"Mrs. Crowther swears that Gene said on his way back to town that he'd see that his wife didn't cause them any more trouble."

"She never caused Father trouble."

"She wouldn't divorce him. That's trouble if you want to marry someone else."

"He didn't want to marry anyone else."

"Mrs. Crowther came out here with your father, and he told your mother . . . Well, you heard it all. You were here."

"When they started quarreling, I left."

"Your mother and your father?"

"Mother never quarreled with Father. Father and Mrs. Crowther."

"What were they quarreling about?"

"I don't know. I tried not to hear."

"Did your father threaten your mother?"

"No. But Mrs. Crowther did. Maybe Mrs. Crowther killed Mother."

"Mrs. Crowther has an alibi from the minute she got back into town. Your father hasn't."

"Maybe I killed her."

"Don't be blasphemous."

"There were times when I wished she was dead."

"Fortunately, you didn't tell anyone that. And fortunately, she wasn't found dead after you said it. Where did you go when you left the house?"

"I took my bedroll and went out to spend the night in the hills."

"Alone?"

"Sure, alone. I'm no hippie."

"Did anyone see you?"

"I don't know. I didn't see anyone."

"When did you get home?"

"Next day. About noon."

"Was your mother here?"

"No."

"Weren't you alarmed?"

"No. I didn't ask her when I wanted to go someplace, and she didn't ask me."

"Where did you think she was?"

"Uncle Eloy's. Out by San Jacinto. That's where she goes when she leaves for a while. That was Sunday night. I phoned Uncle Eloy on Tuesday. He hadn't seen her."

"Then you called the police?"

"Yes."

"Why didn't you call your father?"

"I didn't know where to find him."

"Did you try his office?"

"They didn't know where to find him."

"And the police couldn't find her when they came?"

"No."

"But you did?"

"Later, yes."

"How did you know where to look?"

"I didn't. I went up there by chance."

"You didn't see your father carry her up there?"

"I wasn't here. I told you that. She was a big woman. How could he carry her up there kicking and screaming?"

"She didn't have to be kicking and screaming when he carried her up. Though he was a strong enough man to have done that if necessary."

"How did he kill her?"

"Who knows? What can you tell from bones that have been stripped bare? He knew that. And he knew that I'd come forward with evidence that some years ago she'd seen me about being buried on a platform."

"Buried on, not killed on."

"Okay. Buried. There must have been a lot of buzzards up around that platform for a couple of days. It's a wonder you didn't notice them."

"This is the time of year buzzards from all over come to these trees."

"To the trees, maybe, but not just to that platform. But you didn't see them?"

"I don't spend my entire time watching buzzards."

Mr. Fosdick took off his glasses again. I don't know why he wore them. When he seemed to want to see something particularly closely, he took them off. He leaned forward and looked at me as if I were a strange animal. Or a page of print in some language of which he knew only a few words. I was standing in front of him. I had never sat down since he came in. I felt more alert standing up. He had stopped swearing. I remembered that when Mother and I had gone to his office there had been no swearing. Perhaps he saved swearing for his social life, but when it came to business, he was all business.

"Did Ted Hughes send you here?" I asked. "Or maybe Mrs. Crowther?"

"You called *me*, remember?"

"I haven't said anything to hurt Father."

"You certainly haven't. I'll tell Ted that. Why don't you go up to see your father?"

"I told you that, don't you remember? He doesn't want to see me. He said he wouldn't talk to me if I came."

"You'd think he'd *want* to see you."

"He's probably ashamed of being in jail. How can they keep a man in jail just because of what some woman says? Probably she was trying to get even with some other woman when she said it."

"They couldn't keep him in jail. Except that the wife's dead, and he said she'd cause them no more trouble. And there's no other explanation. Is there?"

"Maybe not. But don't you feel sorry for him? His wife dead. And the woman he was going to marry, according to you, accusing him of murder. Don't you pity him?"

"My God, yes. He was my good friend. I've shed tears for him. That's more than I've seen you do."

"Well, he wasn't a very good father. Let's face it. He kept me from loving my mother."